Homer Rice
on Triple Option Football

Homer Rice

on Triple Option
Football

by HOMER RICE

PARKER PUBLISHING COMPANY INC.   West Nyack, N.Y.

© 1973 *by*

PARKER PUBLISHING COMPANY, INC.

West Nyack, N. Y.

Library of Congress Cataloging in Publication Data

Rice, Homer. (date)
    Homer Rice on triple option football.

    1. Football--Offense. I. Title.
GV951.8.R5   796.33'22   72-8058
ISBN 0-13-394593-6

Printed in the United States of America

DEDICATION

To my family—

> Phyllis, my wife and Head Coach at the Rice home, and my three lovely daughters, Nancy, Phyllis and Angela, my cheerleaders.

HOW THIS BOOK CAN

MAKE YOU A SUCCESS

During the past several years the topic of conversation among football coaches and fans across the nation has been the Triple Option. Many coaches seek information because they are interested in installing the Triple in their offense. Other coaches debate how to defense this explosive attack, and the curious fan asks questions in wonder at this exciting innovation. Undoubtedly, this interest will continue because of the amazing results the Triple has produced. Each year more and more coaches switch to some phase of the Triple Option. Whether it is utilized in the Wishbone formation, the veer attack, or some other offensive set, the three-way option is here to stay.

Because of this widespread interest throughout the football world, I have written this book to help the coach or fan seeking the information necessary to understand completely the three-way option. This book will become a valuable source of information for every coach regardless of classification. It has been said, "A little knowledge is a dangerous thing." In the case of the Triple Option, if the coach doesn't understand the "little things" that make it successful he will fail. With this in mind I have carefully covered each of the many details necessary to success. Each segment has been analyzed methodically. The formation, line spacing, blocking scheme, quarterback "reads" and all the techniques involved in its proper execution have been included. Unless the coach understands the "little things," he cannot prepare his quarterback to execute the Triple. There are several hidden keys which must be known before the Triple attack can get off the ground.

In addition to the Triple, I have explained how the coach can install the pocket-passing game. When these were put together, it produced one of the most exciting combinations in modern-day football.

The elements of its theory are explained throughout. The plan unfolds, simple but sound. However, it is imperative the coach understand the plan before he attempts to coordinate this balanced attack. Understanding this theory will produce tremendous results. The opponent cannot adequately prepare for both the Triple and the pocket-passing game. Another unique feature is explained in chapter 10 (Check-with-Me and Strategy). The secret of how the offense is called by a simple key from the quarterback is carefully explained. Through this key, the quarterback is able to call the best run or pass for a particular situation.

The Triple, pocket pass, and Check-with-Me combine to form a system that will attract the attention of every coach. It becomes a built-in game plan for the entire season. Complete understanding of these basics and of the teaching aids, drills, supplement plays, and play-action passes described will enable the football coach to develop his own version of the three-way option.

Now the story of the Triple concept can be told without holding back any of the secrets that have made it successful.

Homer Rice

ACKNOWLEDGMENTS

My sincere appreciation to:

- Jack Williams and Susan Strobel for their splendid help in preparing the manuscript;
- My parents, Dr. and Mrs. S. C. Rice, for their spiritual guidance, and to my brother, R. Cecil Rice, for his influence upon my career;
- my high school coach, the late Ewell Waddell;
- my college coach, Swede Anderson;
- my University of Cincinnati coaching staff—Ray Callahan, Leeman Bennett, Ralph Hawkins, Ralph Staub, George Boutselis, Owen Hauck, and Jim Kelly;
- the numerous coaches with whom I have come in contact (I have learned from so many);
- all the fine young men it has been my good fortune to coach.

Contents

4. Mechanics of the Triple Option (continued)

5. Triple Option Drills • 108

6. Triple Play-Action Passes • 121

7. The Triple Supplement • 140

8. The Pocket Pass—Protection and Techniques • 151

9. The Pocket Pass Plan of Action • 172

One

BIRTH OF

THE TRIPLE OPTION

This book deals with the Triple Option, one of football's most colorful and exciting innovations.

There has been great debate over where the Triple Option actually began. It's really not all that important. I do believe, however, that certain individuals should be recognized in behalf of the three-way option and for their contributions to the game of football. To my knowledge, the triple first gained prominence in the state of Texas. Bill Yeoman, Head Coach at the University of Houston, developed the Houston Option or the Veer option to set the stage. Coach Yeoman's teams have been national leaders in offensive statistics many times. Houston has utilized the split backfield with a flanker and split end deployment to demonstrate the power of its option. (See diagram 1-1.)

Next came the 1967 Southwest Conference champion, Texas A & M, coached by Gene Stallings. The Aggies conquered Alabama in the Cotton Bowl on January 1, 1968 with their big weapon, the three-way option. Texas A & M exploited the option from the I-slot formation. (See diagram 1-2.)

In the I-formation, the fullback aligns behind the center and

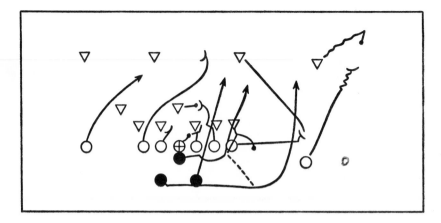

Diagram 1-1

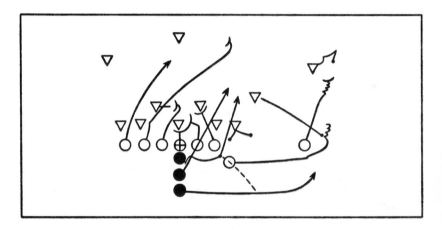

Diagram 1-2

quarterback which differs, of course, from the Houston split backfield. This gives the option a different look.

Then came still another look when Darrell Royal of the University of Texas created the Wishbone-T. (See diagram 1-3.)

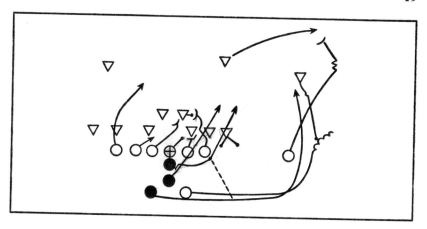

Diagram 1-3

After a slow start in 1968, Texas came on strong to win the Southwest Conference title and post a victory over Tennessee in the Cotton Bowl. The next year, Texas was even stronger—an undefeated team, Southwest Conference champion, winner over Notre Dame in the Cotton Bowl and chief claimant to number one team in the country. National championships are not won by accident. It takes hard work and planning. When the going was tough in the early part of 1968, Coach Royal did not discard the Triple Option. He stayed with it as his basic attack, smoothing out the rough spots to perfection and producing perhaps the strongest team of the decade.

Today, many other top football powers have employed the Houston Veer or the Triple Option (whichever you prefer) adding their intricacies to the innovation and have produced some startling statistics. It can be assumed many more coaches will explore the potential both on the high school and college level. I also predict that someday the professionals will include the Triple in their offensive philosophy. It is because so many coaches and fans across the country have shown such an interest in the Triple Option that I have decided to write this book. I have had such a high number of requests for information that I am compelled to put in writing the complete story of the Triple Option as I understand it. This book of details is needed by the coach interested in installing the Triple Option, for his complete and thorough understanding. Although the Triple is a simple play, the execution of the techniques is so scientific that without complete understanding the coach can do much more harm than good.

The interested fan has heard and read so much about the Triple Option from the sportscasters and writers that this book will afford the fan an opportunity to have almost the same understanding as the coach on the field. If the football fan can follow the game with a technical understanding, he will develop a higher degree of appreciation for the inter-workings necessary to put this great spectacle into operation.

My first experience with the three-way option came in the middle 1950s as a prep coach in Kentucky (Ft. Thomas High). We were highly successful offensively running the Split-T (created by Don Farout of Missouri) and the Inside Belly Series (made famous by Bobby Dodd of Georgia Tech) both in the late 1940s.

If you will go back and study the Split-T and the Inside Belly Series, you will discover that the combination of the two offenses contributed directly to the Triple Option.

SPLIT-T OPTION

Let's examine the Split-T option play first. (See diagram 1-4.) The right halfback drives over his own tackle, faking the handoff. The fake holds the inside segment of the defense and allows a clear-cut option on the defensive end. The quarterback works down the line of scrimmage, carrying out the fake to the right halfback. If the defensive end charges toward the quarterback, the play becomes a pitchout to the swinging left halfback. If the defensive end floats outward, the quarterback keeps the ball and turns upfield. The right offensive end releases downfield on the defensive halfback. He is not required to block on the line of scrimmage since the defensive end will be optioned.

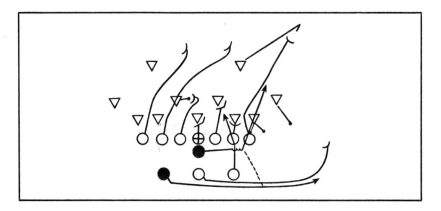

Diagram 1-4

INSIDE BELLY SERIES

Now let's look at the Inside Belly Series. (See diagrams 1-5 and 1-6.) In diagram 1-5, we see the ball handed off to the fullback. The right halfback is utilized as a lead blocker. The blocking for the off-tackle play is changed slightly to encourage the defensive tackle to step to the inside. The right offensive guard and tackle block down with the right halfback blocking on the defensive tackle or the first defender outside the tackle's block. At first this was a simple block for the halfback since the defensive tackle "read" trap and closed to his inside. With the offensive end using a turn-out block on the defensive end, a running lane was created large enough to drive a ten-ton truck through. What a great ball-control series this became along with the Split-T Series! We were having a lot of fun offensively with the execution of the Split-T and Inside Belly against the standard defenses. It wasn't long, however, before defensive coaches re-grouped and decided to slant, loop, and "read" with their interior linemen and we were stymied.

By studying films, we discovered that when we ran the off-tackle play in diagram 1-6 the fullback was breaking through

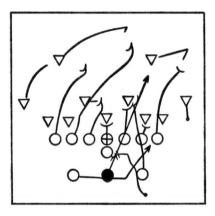

Diagram 1-5

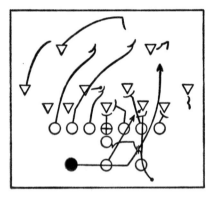

Diagram 1-6

untouched although the ball was thoroughly faked to him with the blocking primarily designed to draw the defensive tackle inside. Therefore, we decided to use the same blocking and give the ball to the fullback (see diagram 1-7), because the defensive tackle was staying at home waiting for the off-tackle play.

Owen Hauck, my line coach at the time, made this strategic discovery and advised not blocking the defensive tackle. As it worked out, we were running both the Fullback Buck and the Off-Tackle with identical blocking rules except for the right end. It became a guessing game for the defensive tackle to decide whether to close down the line to stop the fullback or stay at home for the off-tackle play. Since the defensive tackle was guessing, an additional experiment followed to eliminate any block on the tackle when the Fullback Buck play was called.

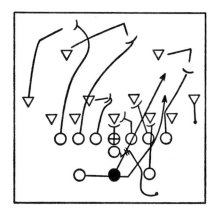

Diagram 1-7

THE FLASH

Since we were running a play called "Flash" (see diagram 1-8) which required the right halfback to swing outside, we decided to assign him this path on the Buck. This gave us a better influence in executing the play, which we determined to make our basic one. (See diagram 1-9.)

Before this innovation, no one ever could have sold me on leaving two defensive linemen free on a straight handoff. That I could be sold indicates the importance of film study. Without it, there would not have been such fantastic developments and progress as have been accomplished by so many in today's modern football.

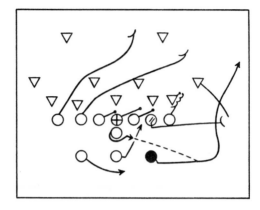

Diagram 1-8

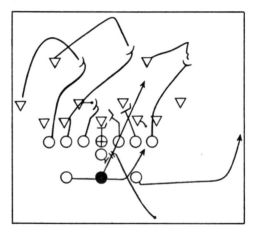

Diagram 1-9

The flaring path of the right halfback held the defensive tackle in check for awhile, but changing defenses, stunts, and continual guessing by the defense made the play an uncertainty.

Unwillingness to give up the Fullback Buck play with the down blocking scheme forced the next step. Could the quarterback "read" the defensive tackle? If he charged toward the ball,

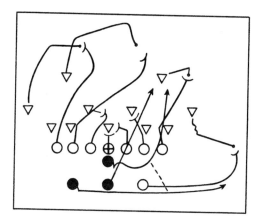

Diagram 1-10

could the Split-T Option be executed? It was developed and the wrinkle became labelled the Triple. (See diagram 1-10.)

THE CONTRIBUTION-TRIPLE

By now you can visualize how the combination of the Split-T and the Inside Belly Series contributed directly to the Triple Option. The fullback replaced the right halfback as the handoff man in the Split-T. The right halfback replaced the fullback as the outside lead blocker for the pitchout. The left halfback carried out the same assignment as when pitch-man in the Split-T. The quarterback now executed part of both series. He started with the handoff to the fullback of the Inside Belly and ended up with the option of the Split-T. It became a three-way option—optioning the defensive tackle for the handoff and the defensive end for the pitch or keep.

This was our football at Highlands High School (Ft. Thomas, Ky.) from 1957 through 1961. Over a five-year period we were undefeated in 50 straight regular season games, state champions in three of the five years and runners-up the other two. We called our offensive football the Short-T formation, but the Triple was the basic play.

As I mentioned earlier, it is not really important how or where the Triple Option began. But while recognizing some of the great coaches that have developed and contributed so much to the game of football, it may be of some interest to recount our experience on the high school level so many years ago. We can claim the name Triple as it has been passed on to others. Through the years, I have discussed with many coaches the execution of this intriguing development. But the Texans (Houston and Texas) have made so much advancement in the three-way option, I sincerely believe the real credit must go to the coaches at those schools.

After my 1961 season at Highlands, I was asked by Charlie Bradshaw to come to Kentucky as the offensive coach. For the next four years (1962-65) we were blessed with personnel who possessed ability in the pocket-passing game. Therefore, I had the opportunity to learn all the details of a complete passing game along with a hard-nose football program. Charlie Bradshaw is one of the great coaches and I owe him a lot for helping me achieve my eventual goal in athletics.

After the 1965 season when our Kentucky offensive unit led the Southeastern Conference in total offense and produced such professionals as Rick Norton, Roger Bird, Sam Ball, Doug Davis, Rick Kestner, Larry Sipel and Bob Windsor, I moved on to Oklahoma as Head Offensive Coach under the late Jim MacKenzie. Jim was another one of the great ones, but a fatal heart attack ended his career at the age of 37. We had experienced an excellent first year (1966) at Oklahoma, beating two of the giants—Texas and Nebraska. Our offensive team established some percentage passing records in the Big-8 Conference. My quarterback, Bobby Warmack, blended to perfection our sprint-out passing game with a strong running game. He later was voted the outstanding player in the Orange Bowl classic when Oklahoma defeated Tennessee.

While at Oklahoma, I often discussed the three-way option with another assistant, Chuck Fairbanks (now Head Coach at Oklahoma). Chuck had previously been with Bill Yeoman at Houston as his offensive coach.

In 1967, I accepted the Head Football position at the University of Cincinnati. I continued to talk to as many people as possible concerning the three-way option. Bud Moore, Texas

A & M's offensive coach, was helpful in explaining their experience with the play.

In the spring of 1968, I made the decision to utilize the Triple Option. I have been involved in offensive football for many years—studying, doing research, thinking, planning, striving toward that perfect attack. At one time, I believed strictly in the strong running game with the sprint out and play-action passes. Then I became intrigued with the pocket pass with sweeps and traps. What I really wanted was a straight-ahead running game and the pocket pass.

The straight-ahead running game became the Triple Option. After high school coaching, offensive coaching at Kentucky and Oklahoma, and after discussing the three-way option with a large number of successful coaches throughout the country, I developed with my very capable Cincinnati staff the 1968 version of the Triple Option.

One of the highlights of this period was the opportunity to discuss the Triple with Darrell Royal of Texas. His concept of all the Triple principles has to be put in the highest category.

Playing one of the toughest schedules in the history of the University of Cincinnati, we produced a winning season the first year we used the Triple Option, led the nation in passing (8th in total offense), averaged 442.1 yards per game, scored over 30 points per game, broke 58 school records, seven NCAA records, produced the leading scorer in the nation in receiver and placekicker Jim O'Brien (now with the Baltimore Colts), and the most valuable player in the 1969 College-Pro All-Star Game, quarterback Greg Cook (now with the Cincinnati Bengals).

Two

COORDINATING THE TRIPLE
WITH THE POCKET PASS

The decision I made to combine the Triple Option with the Pocket Pass turned out to be the most profitable decision I have ever made in offensive football. The combination of the straight-ahead running game and the drop back pass presents the greatest problem a defense can ever face. It is almost impossible for a defensive front to stop a straight-ahead running game while rushing the passer. If the defense prepares to stop the Triple, it cannot be successful rushing the passer.

Offensive coaches strive for balance in their attack. The triple - pocket-pass combination fits this category completely. Whether the coach wants to lean heavily toward either the running or the passing game, he can easily adapt this scheme into his overall plans. When we are ahead we want ball control. When we are behind, we need a "catch-up" offense. The combination of the Triple and the pocket pass can give us this balance.

I believe in both the running and the passing game. When we are strong in both, we can take advantage of the weakness of the defense. When we specialize in only one phase of the offensive game, we are likely to meet a defense strong against that phase. I do realize personnel sometimes dictates the type of offense we employ, but it is important to strive for the perfect attack. So whether we run first or pass first, we need balance.

Before the Triple Option can be utilized, two very important decisions must be made. First, one must be willing to make the Triple Option the basic running game. Secondly, one must decide upon the formation that will be employed. It is not possible to add the Triple as just another play in the running attack. The intricate details are too involved for limited use. It is important to be willing to start from the beginning and master the basic concept. Before a coach can begin, he must completely understand what he is doing. I have warned many coaches that the Triple can be very discouraging without first mastering all the details.

Once the decision is made to make the Triple Option the basic running game, the next step to consider is the type of formation. If the coach considers most important a strong running attack, I suggest the three-back system. On the other hand, if one wants the drop-back passing game, it is important to spread the defense and utilize only two running backs.

The University of Texas profits from the three-back set in its Wishbone-T formation. Texas has relied heavily on a strong running game.

The University of Houston aligns in a pro-type formation with two backs. Although Houston is also a strong running team, it is capable of using more of a passing game because of its formation.

In combining the Triple and the pocket pass at the University of Cincinnati, I was torn between the two-back and three-back formation. I wanted the three-back for the running game, but when it came to passing, I wanted to spread things out and use only two backs. I liked starting the Triple with the fullback behind the quarterback because this was my thinking many years ago. I also preferred the lead blocker coming from the halfback position because of his relationship to the ball carrier and the timing of the pitchout.

Because the pocket pass was such a strong factor in my overall planning, it was necessary to settle on the two-back formation.

When it all was put together, we devised the formation shown in diagram 2-1. I will refer to it as the Cincinnati formation. The details of this formation will be explained in a later chapter.

THE CINCINNATI FORMATION AND THE PLAN

In diagram 2-1 the formation is set to the right. Since a tight end is not necessary in the blocking scheme for the Triple, we have utilized three wide receivers (two on the formation side) to enhance the passing threat. The backs are set behind the guards to run the Triple to either side.

After the decision to go with the Cincinnati formation, the planning began. The plan became simple, sound, and brought fantastic results.

I can remember back through the years how much time was spent each week on the game plan. Sometimes it took two or three days to get everything together. A football squad can sense this and become confused and frustrated.

Our plan became the Triple Option for our running game and a back-up pass for our basic passing game. It sounds almost too simple to be true. Let me assure you it was true. Because of the simplicity of our planning, we were able to talk more to our players about technique and execution; we had eliminated much of the time spent deciding what plays we would run against our opponent.

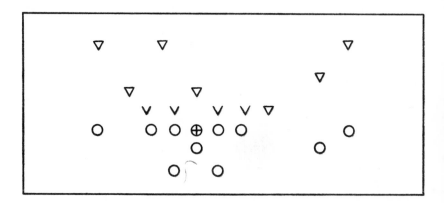

Diagram 2-1

The plan was to line up in the Cincinnati formation with the threat of the pocket pass first and the Triple Option second. Many coaches adhere to the opposite. They believe in the run first, which in many cases results in a passing situation on third down and long yardage. In striving for balance, an offensive team must be a threat both passing and running on each down.

When I say our plan was to line up in a formation with the threat of the pocket pass first, it is because of what the formation, the cadence, and the passing threat do to a defense.

The most important tactical advantage in offensive football is to recognize the defensive alignment and understand its tendencies.

The Cincinnati formation first spreads the defense over the field allowing easy identification. (See diagram 2-2.) The two wide receivers to the right take at least two defenders out of the secondary to that side. With the split of the wide receiver on the left, another secondary man is spread and this gives the remaining safety more area in center field than he is accustomed to handling. With the spread of the four secondary defenders, the defense has only seven men left to cover the wide splits of our line. Therefore, the formation has balanced up the defense to a point that when a weakness occurs it is glaring.

The cadence enters the picture. The threat of the pocket pass is immediate—meaning the ball can be snapped on a quick sound, forcing the defense to line up immediately. It does not give the defense time to disguise or bluff a secondary stunt. This vivid

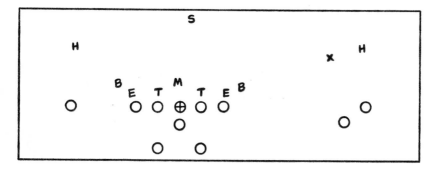

Diagram 2-2

picture simplifies the quarterback's "reads" and "keys" for more effective execution.

If the ball is not snapped on the quick sound and the pocket pass does not take place, the Triple Option and play-action passes enter onto the stage. However, this does not mean the pocket pass will not be used after the Triple or the Triple before the pocket pass. The surprise element in football always enters into the strategy, but it is important to have one basic method of attack. The attitude "we are going to make the first thing we try go whether it is a run or pass," must be established.

Since the defense is always more concerned over long passing, this becomes our initial weapon.

The formation and pocket pass threat forced the defense to tip its hand and this enabled us to maneuver within our system for the best opportunity.

TRIPLE KEYS

In studying the defense versus the Cincinnati formation, let's explore some simple keys which enable the offense to take advantage of defensive alignment.

First of all, in diagram 2-3 locate the safety. The safety can line up in three basic spots. The no. 1 spot indicates the defense is balanced—seven on the front line with four secondary men spaced across the field. We refer to this secondary as "four across the board." The safety's no. 1 position also tips off that coverage could revolve to our left which would enable the defense to be stronger. It would be wiser for the offense to run or pass toward the right.

The safety's no. 2 position is more difficult to determine and depends on the position of the football. If the ball is placed on the left hash mark, the safety is still in position to execute coverage similar to that of position no. 1 because the short side of the field aids in the distance he has to cover. Also, he is a few steps closer to the deep middle of the field. Therefore, the quarterback's job of keying the safety becomes more difficult. To be safe, he should consider running or passing to the formation side, but he also should occasionally run to the left to test the safety's intentions.

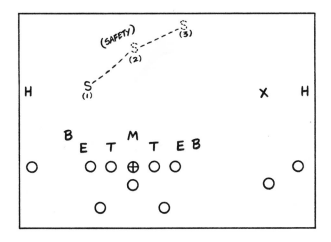

Diagram 2-3

When the ball is in the middle of the field, the spacing becomes too great for the safety when in position no. 2 to be a factor in combination coverage to the offensive left. Therefore, the defense must be considered unbalanced toward the formation side. With this simple reasoning, the quarterback should direct his running or passing game to the left, away from the formation side. However, with the safety in the middle, the quarterback should feel free to go either way because the defense has not moved the safety far enough toward the formation side to indicate a roll-up coverage to the offensive right. In other words, with the ball nearer the middle of the field and the safety in no. 2 position the defense has placed its safety in a vulnerable area. He is neither fish nor fowl.

When the safety aligns in position no. 3, he has indicated possible three-man coverage to our formation side. This gives the quarterback a clear key as in position no. 1. The defense is definitely unbalanced to our formation side and therefore the quarterback must direct his running or passing attack to the left, away from the formation side.

Locating the safety in the defense provides a definite key for the quarterback to determine direction.

After direction is determined, the decision to run or pass can be made by counting the number of defenders on each side.

In diagram 2-4 the safety is aligned in position no. 1, which tells the quarterback to direct the play to the formation side. The defense has moved three defenders out to cover our two receivers. This has weakened the line, leaving only six. Therefore, it is advantageous to execute a running play.

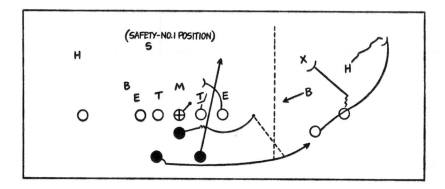

Diagram 2-4

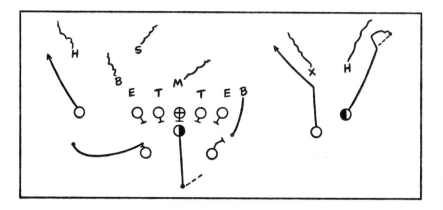

Diagram 2-5

In diagram 2-5 the defense has seven men on the line with only two defenders versus our two receivers on the right. This is a one-for-one situation, and anytime this occurs, we must be able to take advantage of it by passing. All coaches who understand the passing game will work for the one-on-one situation. It is the bread and butter of the forward pass.

The formation has aided the quarterback in knowing the direction for his plays. Also, by counting defenders, he can select a run or pass—the run versus three defenders covering our two wide receivers on the formation side and the pass when only two defenders cover our two. It becomes a simple matter of arithmetic.

When the safety lines up in spot no. 3, the quarterback directs the attack to the left, away from the formation side.

It becomes another mathematical problem with an easy solution. In diagram 2-6, the defense has deployed two defenders to cover our left end. This reduces the front line count to six defenders and indicates we should call a running play.

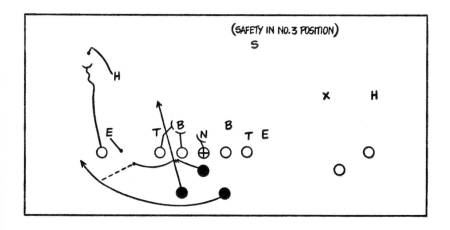

Diagram 2-6

Should the defense keep the seven-man front and cover our left end with one defender, we pass to him. (See diagram 2-7.)

There is a system which enables a team to take advantage of the right play at the right time and this will be explained in a later

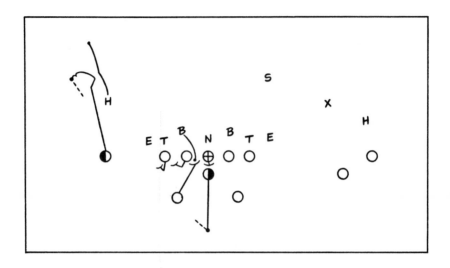

Diagram 2-7

chapter. The system is called check-with-me and enables the quarterback to call the play on the line of scrimmage.

Organization of the pocket pass and the Triple Option must be accomplished by the utilization of one formation, as in the Cincinnati formation which becomes the basic one to execute the combination.

THE BASIC PASS

The basic pass with which to start is 55. This pocket pass has maximum protection if the rush comes, with five potential receivers. The two offensive backs block off the outside line-backers' rush. If they do not blitz, the backs are released into the passing pattern to increase the receivers from three to five.

The entire pocket passing game will be explained in later chapters and broken down into the smallest of details. However, it is important to explain in general the basic pass because this is the game plan to start the passing attack. It is a great plan for a quarterback to work with because he can always depend upon it. If he has problems in other passing schemes, he can always go back to the basic plan.

The basic passing play is tied in with the formation for early and easy identification of the defense. As the quarterback approaches the line of scrimmage with the team he must locate the safety and determine which spot he is occupying. He must determine which side will get the single coverage. The Cincinnati formation and the threat of the pass force the defenders to take their positions quickly because they are aware that the offensive team will report to the line of scrimmage and execute the pocket pass on a quick sound.

In diagram 2-8, the safety has favored spot no. 3 which indicates a strong coverage to the formation side. Before the snap, the quarterback can formulate his decision to drop back and hit his left end because he has the one-on-one coverage.

Basic pass 55 requires the left end to run a sideline pattern. Through trial and error, we discovered this pass to be the most consistent for our basic left end route.

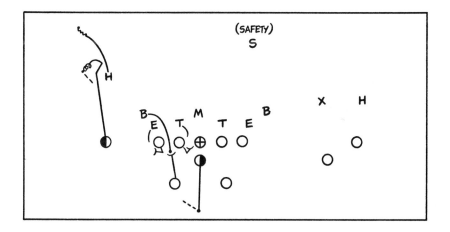

Diagram 2-8

With the defensive safety in spot no. 3, the only way the offensive left end can be double-teamed is for the defense to drop off the outside linebacker on that side. (See diagram 2-9.) We counter this by having our left halfback flare to that side. The

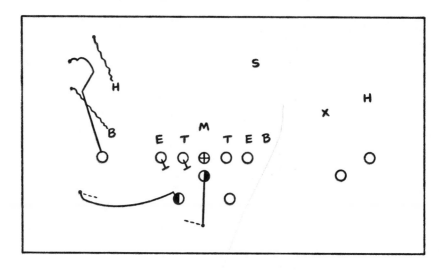

Diagram 2-9

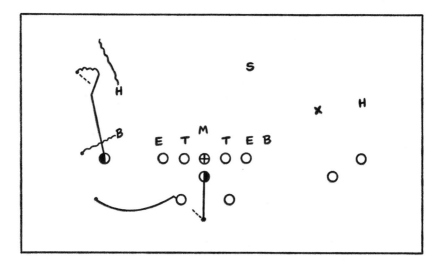

Diagram 2-10

quarterback is aware of this when he sets up. If the linebacker has sprinted into the throwing lane, the quarterback can dump the ball out to his offensive back. If the linebacker covers the offensive halfback, then coverage has been reduced to one-on-one on the end, which allows the quarterback to go with his first intentions. (See diagram 2-10.) The linebacker covering the offensive halfback is not covering in the path of the pass.

As mentioned before, the safety's alignment in spot no. 3 is easy to identify. When the defensive safety lines up in spot no. 1, it could mean many things. The best solution is to direct the pass to the other side, usually to the outside receiver. This man, the right end, runs a post route. This is a deep route and, as I will explain later, the deep route must be executed before any passing game can become successful. Therefore, it is imperative to start with a deep route in our basic passing plan.

When the safety is in spot no. 1 and the coverage turns out to be man-for-man, the deep middle will usually be open for the long pass. This, however, cannot be assumed before the snap. It must be verified by the quarterback as he is dropping back into the pocket. He must "read" the inside safety on the formation side whom we will refer to as the defensive "X" man to determine the type of coverage.

Defensive keys to aid the quarterback are present in alignment before the snap. Other adjustments must be made after the snap. We will refer to these adjustments as "reads."

READING COVERAGE

Our inside receiver (wingback) on the formation side releases inside about nine to 10 yards deep, circling to the inside to an open area. If the "X" man sticks with the wingback, our quarterback can set up and drill the post pass to the right end. (See diagram 2-11.) The quarterback has read man-for-man coverage which puts our right end in a single coverage situation in the deep middle.

Should the defense roll into a zone coverage, our plan would change, because we do not want to throw the football into the deep middle with other people in the area. The best pass would be to our wingback circling to the inside. The wingback works into an open area in the zone by reading linebackers. The wingback's key is the middle linebacker. If the middle linebacker covers the hook zone to our left, the wingback should move into the spot between the middle and the outside linebacker on the formation side. When the middle linebacker covers the hook zone to our right, the wingback must work between the middle linebacker and the outside linebacker to our left.

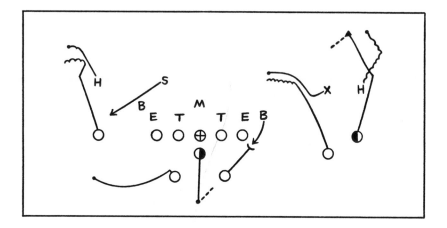

Diagram 2-11

The quarterback has again a simple "read." If the "X" man drops off and does not cover our wingback man-for-man, the secondary has revolved into a zone coverage. In this case, the quarterback sets up and waits momentarily for the wingback to pop open in a middle zone. (See diagram 2-12.)

Only on a few occasions will a defense double-cover the right end with the safety in spot no. 1. In diagram 2-13, the defense doubles our right end with the half back and the outside linebacker. When that linebacker does not rush, our right halfback flares to that side either to reduce the coverage to one-on-one or to be free. After the quarterback gets his key from the safety in spot No. 1, he directs the pass to the formation side and reads the "X" man while retreating into the pocket. The read indicates man coverage, so he sets up ready to drive the ball to the right end. As he is setting up, he discovers the right end is being doubled, so he dumps the ball out to the offensive back just as he

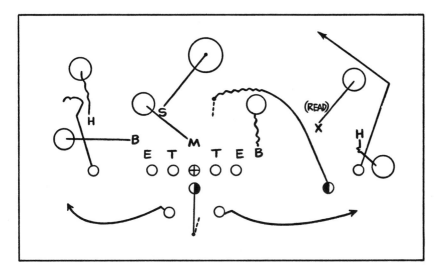

Diagram 2-12

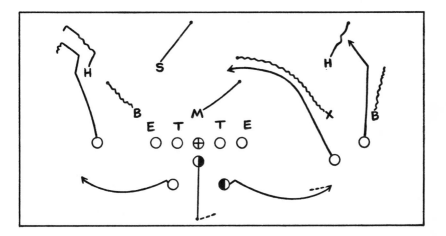

Diagram 2-13

does on the left side when the left end is being doubled. The quarterback, by looking the situation over before the ball is snapped, can be aware of this possibility because of the alignment of the outside linebacker on the formation side.

In one simple plan we can come up with the best pass and the choice route of the five potential receivers by simply calling the number 55 in the huddle.

It should be apparent to the reader how an offensive team can make this the passing plan each week. It is a great plan with which to begin each game. You can get your passing game organized by picking out the various coverages the opponents have decided to employ. Also, as I mentioned before, when something breaks down in the passing game, the quarterback can always go back to the basic plan and start over. I shall never forget a particular game when we were having trouble keeping things going. We almost did not get back to our basic plan soon enough after a fine start. We had fallen behind late in the fourth quarter and became frustrated and started trying this pass and that without any concrete reasoning. My quarterback, Greg Cook, said, "Coach, let's get back to 55." The observation came through loud and clear. Greg did a beautiful job with the key and reading coverages and pulled the game out of the fire. It was a great lesson and enabled me to realize the importance of having a plan upon which you can always rely.

There are many other details of the passing game, but I will explain these complexities in a later chapter. I merely want to illustrate the basic passing plan in order to associate it with the Triple Option running attack.

APPLYING THE TRIPLE

It should be recognizable now how important is the threat of the pocket pass. Now apply the Triple Option as part of the basic plan.

The formation, wide splits in the line, and the pocket pass threat have the defense spread out across the field. The quarterback barks signals on the line of scrimmage, the offensive line is down and, after a tricky cadence, the ball is snapped and here comes the Triple Option.

The blocking is simple and allows the offensive linemen to roll off the line of scrimmage with confidence and expert technique. Their assignments will be explained later but in diagram 2-14, the

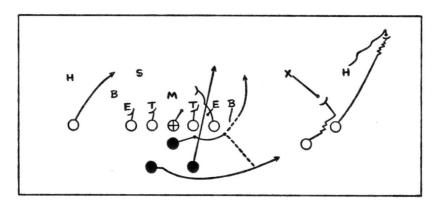

Diagram 2-14

center, right guard, and right tackle have a three-on-two blocking situation where the handoff occurs. The left guard and tackle block the two linemen on their side. The left end checks out the quick throwback passing area while the wingback and right end block the two secondary men on their side of the field.

This blocking scheme has left two defensive men on the line of scrimmage untouched. This portion of the triple concept is the most amazing wrinkle ever developed in offensive football. Blocking strong to the inside and leaving two linemen isolated to be optioned increases the strength of this play to the maximum.

The right halfback drives hard between the offensive right guard and tackle, forcing the defender over the outside shoulder of the tackle to commit. If he commits to the inside to stop the handoff, the quarterback keeps and moves to the next defender. If this defender commits to stop the quarterback, he pitches out to the left halfback, who turns upfield behind two downfield blockers. If the defender plays the pitch, the quarterback keeps and turns upfield for a sizable gain.

The triple can be executed to either side with the same assignments and techniques. Running the triple to the formation side is numbered 71. When it is executed away from formation, it is numbered 79.

With passes 55 and triples 71 and 79 in the Cincinnati

formation, the coach has his, built-in game plan. Also, as far as I am concerned, he has almost a complete offense. Whatever is added must back up the pocket pass and the Triple.

In the following chapters the details of this plan will be thoroughly explained. The little things make the difference in winning or losing. Study them, apply carefully and you will develop the winning edge.

Three

THE TRIPLE

NOMENCLATURE

Before the mechanics and actual operation of the Triple can be described, we must first define the Triple nomenclature. It involves organization of the formations, line spacing, numbering system, play calling, cadence, the pre-stance, and defensive recognition.

Unless detailed concentration is given to this nomenclature, it is impossible to teach the technical phase of the Triple.

FORMATIONS

In chapter two, I disclosed my reasoning for going to the combination of the triple and the pocket pass. In organizing this combination, I mentioned the development of the Cincinnati formation as the basic formation. The Cincinnati formation adhered to flip-flop principles in order to utilize the personnel that best fit the needs for our offense.

Diagram 3-1 illustrates the formation called "Right." In diagram 3-2, the "Left" formation is illustrated. This is as simple a pair of terms as can be used—"Right" and "Left." The formation placed the personnel in the best position to execute the Triple and the pocket pass. It is simple to call and simple to place.

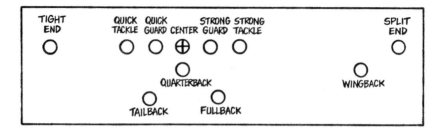

Diagram 3-1

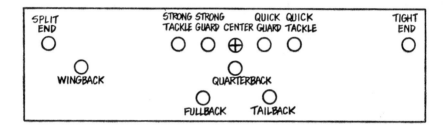

Diagram 3-2

Actually, the Cincinnati formation served our needs for both the Triple and the pocket pass, but for security measures, we had in our repertoire the "I" formation. This formation puts the fullback and tailback in the "I" set and closes the wingback and tight end to within a yard of the tackles. When this formation was set to the right, it was called "Rip." When set to the left, it was called "Len." (See diagram 3-3.) By using a different word rather than adding a word to *Right* or *Left*, we have not prolonged the quarterback's calls.

There are times when the coach will want to have the wingback or tight end or both in tight or set in their wide basic positions. Without making up other formations, this can be handled very easily. It can be understood on certain plays that the wingback or tight end should line up wide or close. If it becomes a problem the receiving coach can signal from the sideline where he wants them.

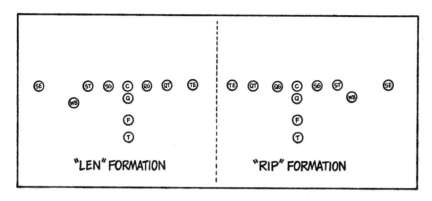

Diagram 3-3

Any other formation needed for a particular game can be given a special name and added without difficulty. In 1968, we went through the entire season at Cincinnati adding very few to the basic formations.

SPACING

Unless the exact spacing of the Cincinnati formation can be adhered to, please do not attempt to execute the Triple with the pocket pass. The spacing is most important and must be understood completely.

The interior linemen (guards and tackles) split one yard; the guards are one yard from the center, the tackles one yard from the guards. Before you assume what one yard may be, measure it out with a yardstick or ruler. Place the yardstick (36 inches) between the near foot of the center and that of the guard. You will be surprised how much space a yard is. Do the same thing between the guard and tackle. When the splits have been settled upon, the distance between the outside foot of the tackles will be nine yards. It can be seen that the interior linemen have covered a lot of ground. This is important in the execution of the Triple. The wide splits stretch the defensive interior to the point where the Triple can cause maximum damage.

If the coach decides upon a tighter formation with a three-back system such as the Texas Wishbone, I recommend narrower splits. The Cincinnati formation spreads the entire defense, stretching the secondary to the breaking point also.

Both ends are instructed to split 12 to 14 yards from the tackles, but must adhere to an eight-yard boundary rule. This means they shall never align any closer to the sideline than eight yards because of their pass patterns. Eight yards allows an end to make all his pass cuts without running out of room on the sideline. Since the ball is placed on the hash mark 70-75 percent of the time, the formation is normally set to the wide side to give the split end and wingback room. The tight end, in most cases, takes his alignment from the boundary (eight yards). With the ball on the hash mark, this puts him approximately five yards from his quick tackle. The split end must adjust his position more often. He must first adhere to the eight-yard boundary rule but get as far from the strong tackle as ability will allow. The ability factor is determined by the speed of the split end and the strength of the passer on the deep sideline cut. If he can drive the football without hanging it up, the split end should take the maximum split. The weaker the throwing arm, the tighter the split. Jim O'Brien, our crack split end at Cincinnati, found 19 yards from the ball to be the best width with Greg Cook throwing from the other end. With the ball on the left hash mark and our split end set a yard outside the right one, the pass traveled 30-yards from where the quarterback set up in the pocket to the hands of the receiver at the end of the sideline cut.

When the tight end was called upon to line up tight, his spacing was one yard from the quick tackle.

The wingback takes his basic spacing from the split end. When the huddle breaks, the wingback follows the split end and lines up four to five yards to his inside and one yard deep. The spacing of the split end and the wingback serves the purpose of spreading the entire defense.

When "Rip" or "Len" formation is called the wingback lines up one yard outside the strong tackle and one yard deep.

The position of the fullback is four yards deep behind the strong guard in the "Right" and "Left" formation; in the "Rip" and "Len" formation he moves behind the center.

The depth of the tailback is also four yards in the"Right" and "Left" formations and his alignment is directly behind the quick guard. When "Rip" or "Len" formation is called, he moves one yard behind the fullback.

Diagram 3-4 illustrates the basic spacing for "Right" formation from the left hash mark. Diagram 3-5 illustrates spacing of "Rip" formation.

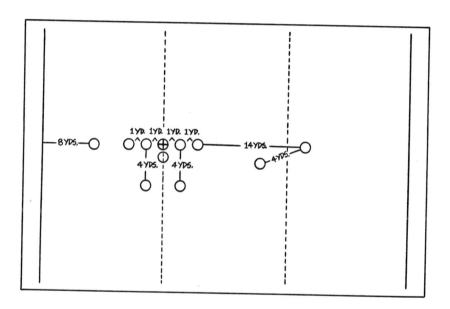

Diagram 3-4

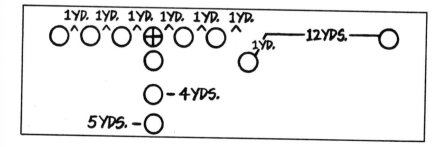

Diagram 3-5

Another important item in the Triple and the pocket pass is for the guards and tackles to line up as deep as possible on the line of scrimmage. The forward point of a lineman's stance must be within one foot (12 inches) of the neutral zone—the length of the football. (See diagram 3-6.) The center is allowed to have his head over the ball. All other linemen, both defensive and offensive, are allowed up to the imaginary line on their side of the neutral zone. In order to take full advantage of these rules, we instructed our linemen to line up eleven inches from the neutral line. To gauge the proper alignment, the guards lined up their shoulder pads on the feet of the center. The tackles lined up the same depth as the guards. This alignment procedure takes a little preparation but is well worth the time. As long as the hand or head of the guard or tackle in his down stance did not exceed the one-foot rule either way, the position was perfect. When the lineman was in a pre- or upright stance, he was able to judge the distance by lining up his feet behind the center's.

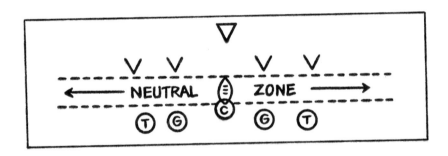

Diagram 3-6

The purpose of deeper alignment is twofold. In the triple, the lineman wants to be off the ball so he can read the defense. The offensive lineman knows when the ball will be snapped and where he is going. He can see the defense react as he is coming off the line of scrimmage to execute his block. The timing is also better for the handoff, keep, or pitch of the triple. The other main purpose involves blocking for the pocket pass. In protecting the passer, the offensive lineman wants to delay his block as long as possible because of the time factor. The closer to the neutral zone the more advantage the defensive rusher has. He can play off the blocker and have a clear path to the quarterback.

The exact spacing and alignment are vital ingredients in the success of the offensive plan. The prescribed alignment is basic and will be changed from time to time. This will be explained in later chapters, but starting from the beginning, one must learn the basic position to have a base to start operation.

NUMBERING SYSTEM

The numbering system of the Triple is also simple. We number from one through nine. Starting with the split end in "Left" formation, we number 1-2-3-4-5-6-7-8-9 as indicated in diagram 3-7. Each position keeps the same number. The split end has no. 1, the wingback no. 2, and so on across the line of scrimmage. When the formation is set to the right such as "Rip" formation, the numbers flip-flop over. (See diagram 3-8.)

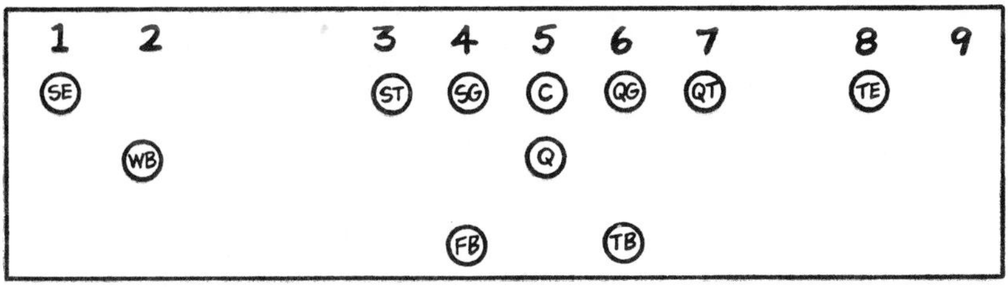

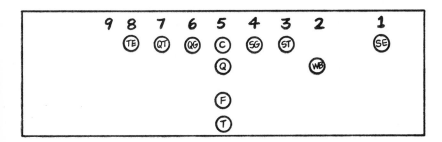

Diagram 3-7

Diagram 3-8

When a number is called in the huddle it represents the point of attack, which means the ball carrier will be running toward number one, number four, number nine, etc. This number is always the last digit called in the huddle.

All the basic plays are numbered. This makes them simple to call, simple to understand, and is a very uncomplicated way to signal a play from the sideline. The numbers are in two digits, such as 71, 79, 92, 93, or 98, with the first number indicating the type of backfield action.

Seventy-one indicates that backfield action is the triple option with the point of attack directed toward the split end. The ball may not actually get out to the no. 1 position because in the Triple the handoff or quarterback keep may occur before the pitch. But for simplicity, we always used the widest possibility of the play for the point of attack. (See diagram 3-9.)

The last number also describes to the offensive line the type of blocking to execute. Having only one block for each number helps the coach keep simplicity in his attack.

The double-digit system controls the play, the block, and the point-of-attack. It also limits the blocking scheme to one through nine. Should any other play be added from time to time, it would have to be given a special name.

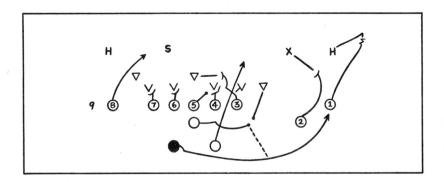

Diagram 3-9

PLAY CALLING

Play-calling by the quarterback can be done either in the huddle or on the line of scrimmage. On the line of scrimmage, calls benefit the team when time is running out in the first or second half of the game or for automatic purposes. This element will be discussed in a later chapter.

After the huddle is formed, the quarterback steps into it facing his team's bench. The center commands, "Now," which starts concentration on the play to be called. The quarterback either receives a signal from the sideline or calls the play on his own. He will first call the formation, then the play number twice, then the cadence. The cadence indicates when the ball will be snapped.

An example of a call by the quarterback is—"Right" 71-71 on third sound. "Right" is the formation, 71 is the play. Seventy-one is repeated to insure that each member heard and understands, then the snap count or cadence is pronounced. The cadence can be on the quick sound or the first, second, third, or fourth sound.

The quick sound means the ball is snapped while the team is in the pre-stance position and before any audible or other calls are made. The first, second, third, or fourth sound follows the audible call.

ON THE LINE

The quarterback's call on the line of scrimmage starts with the quick sound—"Hike." It is followed by the audible system—twenty-two, twenty-two. Any number can be used as long as the call is dummy. The audible is only live when the quarterback so instructs his team in the huddle or lines the team up without a huddle. This system will be completely explained in the chapter on Check-with-me. The first sound "Hike," the second sound "Hike," the third sound "Hike," and the fourth sound "Hike," follow the audible or dummy call. The ball can be snapped on the quick sound, first, second, third, or fourth sound, whichever the quarterback decides upon in the huddle call. An example of a call on the third sound is, "Hike, twenty-eight, twenty-eight, Hike,

Hike, Hike." The quick sound was called, then the audible or dummy numbers, then the first "Hike," second "Hike," and finally the third "Hike," upon which the ball is snapped.

The quarterback calls the play in the huddle, and the split end, center, tight end, and wing back leave it. Then the quarterback breaks the huddle—"Break and go." The team sprints to the line of scrimmage and lines up in a pre-stance. This means the guards and tackles take their positions in a two-point stance. The tailback and fullback also take a two-point stance but place their hands on their knees for a higher position. The pre-stance position for the linemen and backs correlates with the quick sound. Earlier, I explained how the pocket passing game became the first threat to the defense because it could happen on the quick sound. The pre-stance is the best position to be in for protection of the passer, therefore the pre-stance, the quick sound, and the pocket pass correlate for the big threat.

The split end, wingback, and tight end should be in a down position. The down position is the best position for a quick start. Therefore, for receivers to accelerate from the line of scrimmage, we instructed the down position always for the split end, wingback, and tight end.

When the ball was not snapped on the first sound, the guards, tackles, tailback, and fullback dropped into a down position. Also, if any position had to move, it was done at this time. If the wingback or tight end was involved in a play which called upon him to be tight and he was set wide, this meant he must get up and move quickly to that position. If the tailback or fullback had to move his position either to the "I" set or to another position, it had to be done at this time.

Since the rules will not permit the offensive guards and tackles to move once they have taken a down stance, it makes sense to approach it from a pre-stance to a down stance.

THE CADENCE

The cadence became another very important item in the Triple offense. For years I had believed in only a single sound. The ball was always snapped on the same count and although we thought it

was a non-rhythm, it was not. It became rhythm because we
always used the same sound. We believed, of course, the single
sound would eliminate the offsides penalty and the problem of
concentration. It did this, but it also aided the defense. All
coaches understand that the defense reacts to the movement of
the ball or an offensive player. Although the defense is taught not
to hear the sound, it is almost impossible to completely eliminate
this. When the offense uses a single sound, it is not long before the
defense begins to charge on the sound rather than movement.

The cadence should control the defense. By varying the
counts, the offense can accomplish this. Also, by associating
certain counts with certain parts of the offense, something like the
single sound controlling offsides and aiding concentration can be
achieved. Examples of this are the pocket pass on the quick sound,
the Triple and all automatics on the third sound, and the "I" set
on the first sound, etc.

The defensive charge can be controlled by variations of the
count and by voice range. For example, the quarterback has called
in the huddle—"Right, seventy-one, seventy-one, on the third
sound." The team goes down on the quick sound and the
quarterback makes a dummy audible call (twenty-six, twenty-six)
and shouts the cadence—Hike-Hike-Hike. The ball is snapped on
the third Hike. But the second Hike was different from the first
Hike. The voice was higher and stronger. This effects the defense
and sometimes the defensive front will surge. When it surges, the
weight is rocked forward and the defense becomes over-extended.
While the defenders are rocking back, the third Hike is called and
the offensive lineman rolls off into the defense while the defenders
have their weight back on their heels. The change of voice range
by the quarterback is not intended to pull the defense offside.
Although this happens frequently, it is intended to control the
defensive charge because a front-line defender will commit to
sharp sounds by surging forward, destroying the timing of a
defensive charge. The perfected cadence will control the defensive
charge and allow the offensive line to move the front defenders off
the line of scrimmage.

Looking back through films, I have witnessed some of our
offensive linemen blocking a defensive guard or tackle 10 to 15

yards downfield. Anytime one player has his weight rolling forward making contact with an opponent with his weight settling backwards, the outcome is obvious.

DEFENSIVE RECOGNITION

Recognizing defenses and defensive tendencies is another vital area of successful offensive planning. When the player knows whom to block, the coach can spend valuable time teaching the technique of blocking. When a player is confused on his blocking assignment, then he is not aggressive. An offensive line cannot be confused. It must be aggressive. Understanding this theory makes the coach realize the importance of defensive recognition.

In combining the Triple with the pocket pass, the defensive recognition was handled by a combination of terminology. Actually it involved two methods. One method is numbering the defensive positions. The other method is describing the defensive position. In essence, we are attempting to organize a rule for each assignment that would be short, descriptive, and provide a quick communication system between coach and player and between player and player.

DEFENSIVE NUMBERING

The numbering system starts with the defensive position over the center. This number was zero. Then by counting each position to the right, one-two-three-four, and to the left, one-two-three-four (see diagram 3-10), we were able to establish a position count.

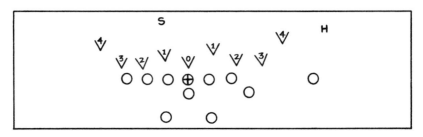

Diagram 3-10

The secondary was always named. Regardless of whether the secondary was three or four defenders, we read quickside to strongside. Three defenders is simple—halfback, safety, halfback. Four defenders was read left to right—halfback, safety, "X," halfback. (See diagram 3-11.)

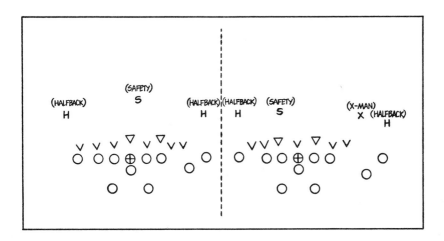

Diagram 3 11

In diagram 3-12, I have illustrated the numbering system versus twelve defenses. It is possible to create hundreds of defensive arrangements, but it is only necessary to describe the twelve defenses in diagram 3-12 because all situations are covered for the offensive linemen.

When double numbers occur such as the stacks and splits, it depends upon which way the play is directed to determine the blocking number. For example, a play is called toward the formation with the strong guard assigned to block no. 1 and the right tackle no. 2. The front defender in this case becomes no. 1 and the linebacker no. 2. (See diagram 3-13.) However, if the play is called away from the formation with the same assignments, the front defender becomes no. 2 and the linebacker no. 1. (See diagram 3-14.)

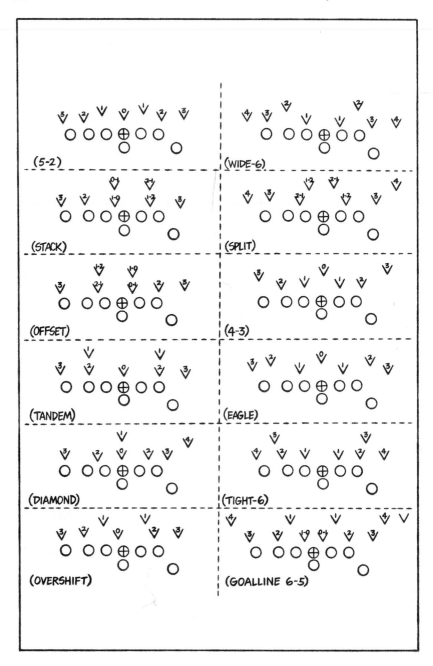

Diagram 3-12

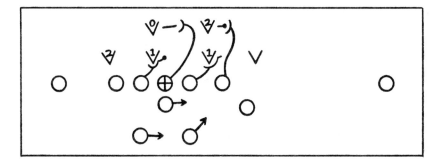

Diagram 3-13

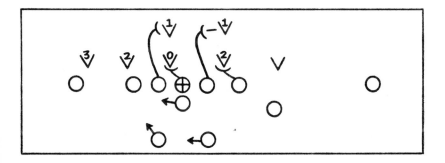

Diagram 3-14

The numbering system can also be utilized to count only the defensive linemen excluding linebackers. This system is commonly used in the pocket pass protection rules. In diagram 3-15, the guards are assigned no. 1 on the line of scrimmage and the tackles no. 2.

The initials LOS abbreviate line of scrimmage to shorten the assignment. The strong assignment could read for a particular pass series "no. 1 LOS," which would be descriptive of the strong guard's assignment and would serve as a communication system throughout the squad. If his assignment in diagram 3-15 was no. 1, he would be blocking on the linebacker instead of the defensive left tackle, which is No. 1 LOS.

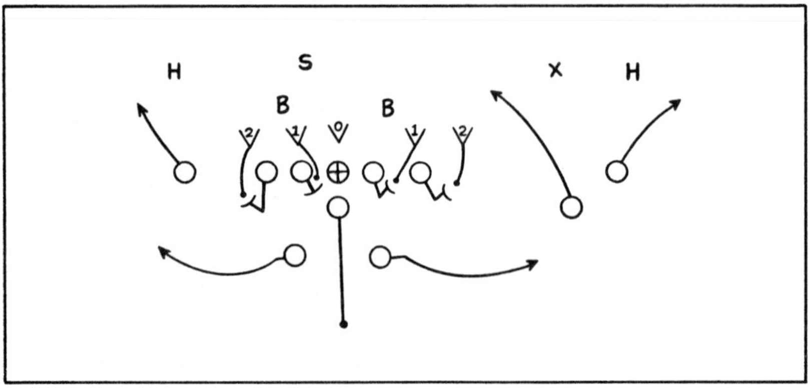

Diagram 3-15

DEFENSIVE POSITIONS

The method which describes the defensive position involves explaining to the offensive lineman the different positions in which a defender can line up in his blocking area. This method is necessary to explain the counting system anyway. After the player understands the several defensive positions in his area, then he can apply a number to that defender regardless of his alignment. When an assignment involves both a number and a defensive position description because of the nature of the defense, then the defensive position method is applied for the rule.

For example, the strong tackle is to block a defender in his inside gap; if no one lines up in the inside gap, he blocks the first inside linebacker. In diagram 3-16, one part of the illustration shows the strong tackle blocking the defender in the inside gap, no. 2, while the other shows him blocking the linebacker, no. 1, in another situation. Therefore, two numbers are involved, so it is necessary to use a position description.

We refer to defensive positions in an individual blocking area as "looks." The center's area has as many as six "looks." The defender can line up in either gap, on his nose, as a single linebacker, as one of double linebackers such as in a split defense, or no one may line up in the area such as in the wide-6 defense.

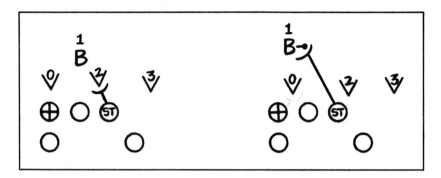

Diagram 3-16

The center must know whether the play is directed toward the strong side or the quick side. In diagram 3-17, assume the play has been called to the strong side with the formation set to the offensive right.

The guard, tackle, tight end and wingback must also understand defensive positions in their blocking areas. The defenders can line up in the inside gap, outside gap, directly over, shaded inside shoulder, shaded outside shoulder, or as a linebacker. (See diagram 3-18.)

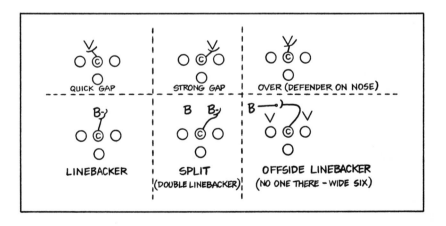

Diagram 3-17

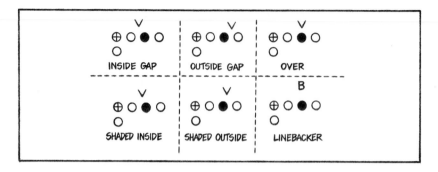

Diagram 3-18

Beyond each individual understanding the single defensive position in his blocking area, he must also understand defensive-front alignments such as stacks, tandems, splits, offsets, etc. These are referred to as defensive front "looks." Each player must be able to recognize and understand the basic defensive-front looks as illustrated in diagram 3-12.

Sometimes determining whether a front-line defender is on or off the line of scrimmage is difficult. Therefore, we made the distinction between the defensive line and linebackers. A defender was considered a linebacker if he was one-yard off the line of scrimmage and lined up in a two-point stance. Anyone within a yard of the line of scrimmage, whether he was in a two-, three-, or four-point stance, was considered a defensive lineman.

In summary, recognizing defenses involves numbering and recognizing the defensive position. In organizing blocking rules for each play, we gave the player a short assignment which is a summary of recognizing and understanding the complete picture. The assignment tells him whom to block. There will be coaching points beyond this for how to attack his assignment and be aware of the different tendencies and stunts his assignment may perform.

The defensive recognition phase is well worth the time to study and completely understand it because only after the blocker understands whom to block, can he be taught the technique of blocking. This is where the offensive game is won or lost.

All in all, the nomenclature prepares us to start the center's snap to the quarterback which leads into the really exciting phases coming up in chapter four.

Four

MECHANICS OF

THE TRIPLE OPTION

The Triple is the most intriguing development I ever have been associated with in my football career. The Triple Option is the heart of this book and now it is time to put it all together by describing the mechanics from the theory down to the tiniest detail.

Chapter one explained the background, chapter two presented the theory of the Triple - pocket-pass combination, and chapter three explained the nomenclature to bring us to the point, where we can get into the workings of the Triple.

PLAY 71

As mentioned earlier, when the Triple is called toward formation, it is numbered 71. When it is called away from formation to the quick side, it is numbered 79. Therefore, from this point on, we will refer to 71 and 79 as the Triple.

Let's start with 71. First, each offensive position has an assignment. The assignment briefly explains the blocking rule or backfield duty. The brief explanation is the communication system between coach and player and between player and player. It allows communication by short terms of defensive recognition, who should be blocked and what the back's path must be, etc. After this understanding, the coach can get into the technique phase—but not before.

A rule sheet on each play is placed in the coach's notebook with this information. For 71, the rules are broken down by position:

Split End	—	Deep 1/3
Wingback	—	Short outside 1/4
Strong Tackle	—	Inside gap, linebacker
Strong Guard	—	#1
Center	—	#0
Quick Guard	—	#1
Quick Tackle	—	#2
Tight End	—	Check 24—Deep middle 1/3
Quarterback	—	Execute Triple principle
Fullback	—	Hand-off
Tailback	—	Pitchout

THE SPLIT END

The split end's assignment is deep 1/3. This means he must block the secondary defender covering that area of the field. After the split end understands his assignment, the receiving coach can now work on the technique. The coach must instruct his split end to release exactly as he does on the basic pass patterns, pushing the defensive halfback downfield. When the defensive back recognizes the play is a run and starts upfield, the split end must move into his path. The worst thing the split end can do is to attempt to block the defender too soon. The split end must take short, jabby steps staying between the defender and the ball carrier (assuming the ball has been pitched to the tailback) similar to a defensive player guarding an offensive player in basketball. If the split end attempts to block too soon, the timing factor will be destroyed and the defensive back can easily come up and make the play if the ball is pitched out to the tailback. The split end must delay his block as long as possible and continue to push the defender downfield as far as possible. The better job the split end does on his release, the easier his assignment can be accomplished. Once the defensive back makes a break for the ball carrier, the split end must attack the far hip of the defender with a roll-block technique.

The roll-block technique will be used by all our backs and wide receivers for downfield and corner-blocking. The roll block is a snapping, twisting block that is thrown around the ankles. If the defender breaks to the split end's left, the split end will throw the back of his right shoulder into the right hip of the defender. As contact is made, the split end should swing his left elbow upward to start his roll. He must roll at least three times to perfect the block. A well-executed roll-block accomplishes the assignment regardless of how the defender plays. If he plays off the blocker, he must back pedal with his hands on the blocker which allows the ball carrier to break downfield with an opportunity to break off the split end's block. If the defender does not use his hands, he will invariably go down if the split end does his job. Of course, when he goes down, the ball carrier is by him for the big play.

Again, let me point out it is very important for the split end to delay his block as long as possible. He could make a perfect block and the defender could get off the ground and still make the play on the line of scrimmage. The split end must be a good actor by encouraging the defender to think deep pass. Then, he must make every effort to stay on his feet and in front of the defender. If he face-guards him properly, it will affect the defender's vision. With the split end in his face, he will not be able to see the play.

THE WINGBACK

The wingback has the most difficult block. His assignment is the short outside 1/4. His assignment must be correlated with the split end's. At least two defenders will always line up opposite the split end and wingback. As the split end releases off the line of scrimmage into the deep 1/3 area, one of the two defenders will cover that area whether it is the halfback or X man (inside safety). The remaining defender will cover the short outside 1/4 of the field. Once the wingback recognizes his assignment, he must apply the appropriate technique.

The wingback must also delay his block. The best timing for this block occurs from a halfback position such as the Wishbone T. Therefore, to compensate for the width of the wingback's position necessitates the delay. The wingback, by alignment, is already in position to execute the block, but must delay at least two seconds before actual contact is made. In diagram 4-1, the defensive halfback covers the deep 1/3 with the X man covering the short outside 1/4. The wingback must delay the two-second count and gain an outside position. The outside position keeps the outside running lane open for the back to break down the sideline. The wingback is instructed to use the roll-technique block as described for the split end.

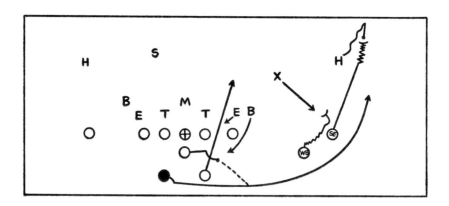

Diagram 4-1

Should the defensive halfback come up to cover the short outside 1/4 and the X man take the deep 1/3, the split end and wingback must switch assignments. In recognizing this the wingback should still delay the two counts, then sprint toward the defensive halfback attacking the far hip with a roll block. In this case the ball carrier would normally cut inside the wingback's block as designated in diagram 4-2.

These are the basic assignments for the split end and wingback for 71. However, because of the complexities of defenses, down

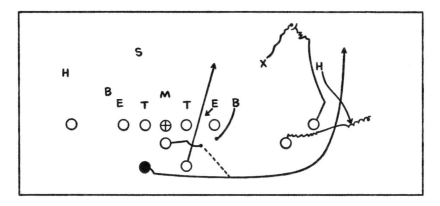

Diagram 4-2

and distance situations, and certain areas on the field, we employed three other methods at Cincinnati.

One of the three occurred in our goal-line offensive plan. Because of the lack of room inside the opponent's five-yard line, we taught a crossblock. To accomplish this, we lined up our wingback a yard outside our strong tackle. The split end cracked back on the X man while the wingback sprinted laterally to use a roll block on the defensive halfback. (See diagram 4-3.) The crossblock is the best timing device in this area because the split end and wingback can sprint into their blocks without any delay. Because of the lack of space, the crossblock can be effective.

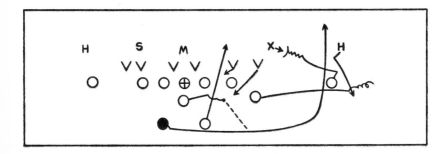

Diagram 4-3

The second method came about by experimenting on a third-down situation with more than five yards to go. Since the defense is thinking so strongly of pass, the split end and wingback both release downfield to soften the corner. Normally, the defense will align three defenders to cover the two wide receivers on our split end side. In diagram 4-4, the wingback and split end sprint deep, taking two defenders with them and leaving only one defender to play the option.

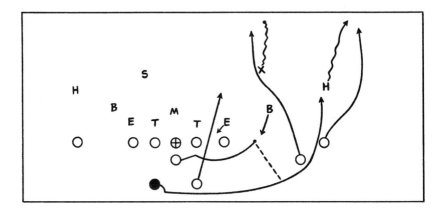

Diagram 4-4

In diagram 4-5, the third method is illustrated, another blocking method developed from an experiment. Because of our strong passing game, some of our opponents played the two-deep safety with five short defenders playing our ends, wingback, fullback, and tailback man-for-man.

We did some screening for certain pass patterns against this type of defense and the blocking scheme of this type worked out very well. The wingback screened in front of the defender covering our split end, then sprinted downfield forcing the man covering the wingback to "get on his horse" to cover him. The split end loafed off the line of scrimmage for a few steps to allow the screen to be performed, then sprinted to the inside. The defender covering the split end had to fight off the screen, then fly to catch up with the split end. The confusion presented a soft corner for

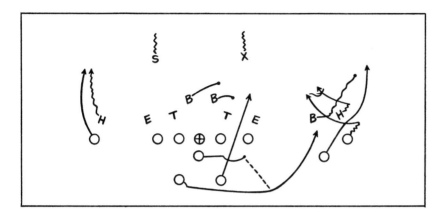

Diagram 4-5

the ball carrier to turn upfield for a big play. Should the defense line up in the two-deep and play zone with the short five, the wingback ends up blocking the defensive halfback and the split end blocks the linebacker.

The assignment and blocking technique described for the split end and wingback are so designed in the event the pitchout occurs. Should the handoff or quarterback keep occur instead, it becomes a matter of reaction to block in front of the ball carrier if possible. The point, however, must be clear—set up the block for the pitchout.

THE TIGHT END

The next position to describe is the tight end's. The receiving coach instructs the split end, wingback, and tight end in regard to pass routes and blocking assignments. Therefore, the sequence to follow in describing the mechanics must be explained by coaching areas.

In most offenses, the tight end aligns on the formation or strong side with a wing or flanker back outside of him. In the Cincinnati formation, he aligns as the end opposite the formation. He is called a tight end because he will at times line up a yard outside the quickside tackle for blocking purposes.

For 71, he wants to split his regular rule. His assignment is to check for a pass called 24, then block into the deep middle 1/3. Twenty-four (24) is a quick throwback pass, shown in diagram 4-6.

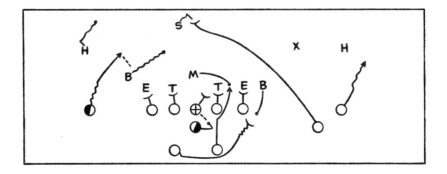

Diagram 4-6

The area becomes vulnerable late in the third and fourth quarter after 71 has been effective. As 71 begins, the linebackers pursue, leaving an area unprotected. It is the duty of the tight end to find this area by experimenting with different releases until he is sure he will be open. Once this is discovered, the quarterback has a quick pass that will be a life-saver late in the game, averaging 15 to 20 yards on each reception. This is the reason the tight end must check this area out when 71 is called. After he checks the area he then must sprint downfield to block in the event the ball carrier cuts back into the deep middle.

THE INTERIOR LINE

The offensive line coach works with the center, strong guard, strong tackle, quick guard and quick tackle. The interior line is the life blood of the offense. The job that is done with this group will determine whether the offense sinks or swims. Therefore, it is imperative to have aggressive football players. Keep the assignments simple so the linemen can spend their valuable time working on technique. This makes the difference between success or failure of the offense.

The blocking scheme for 71 is simple. Let's start with the center. His assignment is no. 0.

THE CENTER

In diagrams 4-7 and 4-8, the reader can follow the center's assignment. We have placed the defensive looks into two categories—the odd front and the even front. In the odd fronts, no. 0 is the nose guard (N), on the line of scrimmage opposite the center's nose. The center has a definite technique for each situation. With no. 0 on his nose, he must assume the nose guard will be playing straight unless he tips his hand before the snap. In any event, the technique the center employs will take care of each situation versus the odd-front defenses. Following diagram 4-7 versus the regular 5-2 defensive look, the center must come off the line of scrimmage aiming for the nose guard's outside leg. I have diagrammed each play to the right for simplicity; therefore, the outside leg of the nose guard will be the left. This means if the nose guard plays a normal defensive technique, the center should make contact with his left shoulder pad just under the nose guard's left kneecap. This point of contact is the perfect spot. However, we must take into consideration the sizes of the nose guard and the center. Also, the height of their stance must be considered. If the offensive center is a tall individual and the nose guard on the short side, the point of contact will naturally be higher on the nose guard. These details must be understood by the offensive line coach in working with each individual. The spot just below the knee cap is perfect and gives a basic point toward which to work.

The offensive coach must always stress the eyes, rolling off the line, and short steps before contact is made. Seeing the target as the cadence is called for the snap must always precede any movement. The center must see the point with which he is attempting to make contact. As the center rolls off the line, taking short steps to keep from rising, his hips will stay closed to allow an explosion when his left shoulder makes contact with the lower part of the nose guard's kneecap. As contact is made with the left shoulder, the left cheek must scrape the outside part of the kneecap to form a V shape or lock around the knee. The center's

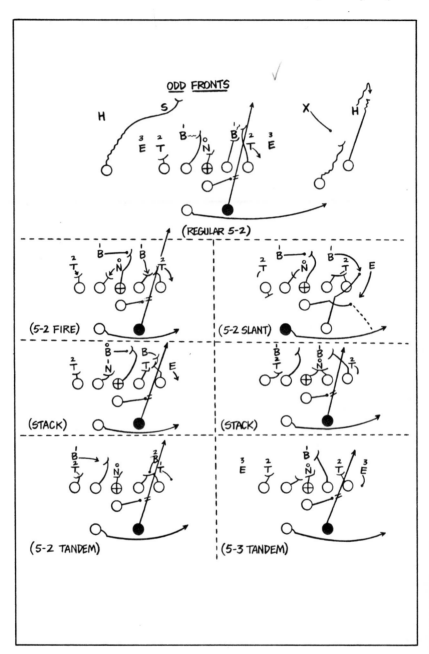

Diagram 4-7

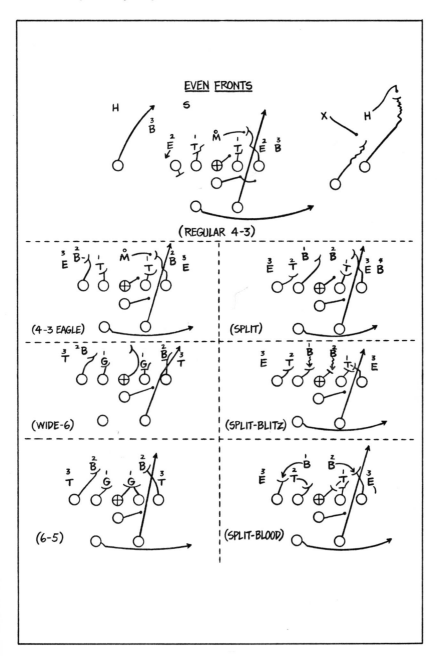

Diagram 4-8

left forearm must be up high to increase the locking base. This is the V of the neck which keeps contact through the bulk of the defender, preventing the blocker from sliding off the corner. As contact is made, the hips tuck under to extend the weight through the defender. From that point on, the blocker must make a second effort for the follow-through. He must stay after the defender until he has moved him off the line of scrimmage. If the blocker dedicates himself to battle for six seconds, he will win the fight. The coaching points in the block must be taught in this sequence: stance, look, roll off, approach, contact and follow-through.

This technique versus a nose guard playing a defensive straight technique will hold up as long as everything is equal. Even if the defensive nose guard is slightly stronger, the center still has an advantage because he knows when the ball will be snapped and has the staggered cadence to help also. Perhaps the biggest advantage is the fact the center is blocking through a spot on the nose guard and is not concerned with losing him to his inside. This greatly aids the center in his effort to be aggressive. Should the nose guard be so strong that the center cannot block him in any way, it is necessary to change the blocking scheme to the double-team block shown in diagram 4-9, where the offensive guard helps the center. This scheme changes the tackle's assignment to a solo block on the linebacker. This type of blocking scheme is more necessary when the back who will carry is set behind the center. With the handoff back moved behind the offensive guard as in the Cincinnati formation, it is very possible the center can maintain his block long enough to keep the nose guard from being a factor regardless of his strength.

I point this problem out so you can understand this possibility. The entire play will be a failure unless the center can get his job accomplished. When the center runs up against the extra strong nose guard, such as Pat James, Oklahoma defensive coach, had in Granville Liggins from 1966-68 then an alternative plan must be available.

When the nose guard plays straight on the center and follows the flow of the play or slants toward the call of the play, the basic technique will hold up under normal circumstances. The change in technique comes when the nose guard slants away from the play or uses the run-around technique made famous by the great

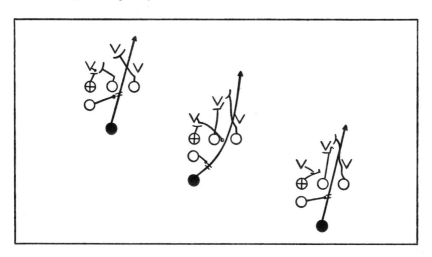

Diagram 4-9

defensive teams of Jim MacKenzie at Arkansas during the late 1950s. Examples of this technique are shown in diagram 4-7, odd fronts such as the 5-2 fire and 5-2 slant. It must be understood that any odd front with the nose guard playing over the center presents this threat.

The center approaches the block the same. He understands he is not responsible for the defender if he slants away; therefore, the center can come off the line of scrimmage very aggressively. The offensive quickside guard steps toward the nose guard enroute to block the linebacker and picks up the nose guard, slanting away from the play. This allows the center to pick up the linebacker. (See diagram 4-10.) Because of the distance the center must travel to pick up the linebacker, the blocking will be higher. The spot now becomes the belt buckle on the linebacker. The center should locate the belt buckle with his eyes and drive his left shoulder into the center point. This spot places the shoulder pad more through the middle of the defender. As the shoulder makes contact, the head slides past the strongside hip. The hips should tuck under as the blocker creates a lifting action with strong leg drive to maintain the block for the required time. The head must come up to maintain the leg drive—"Look for the treetops." Staying with the block is a simple matter of effort if the technique approach is mastered.

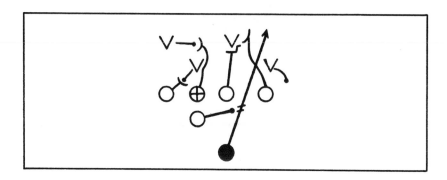

Diagram 4-10

Versus the even fronts, the center has three different looks. One linebacker, two linebackers, or no one at all lined up in the zero area. Regardless of which type he faces, the center must step through the strong gap. (See diagram 4-11.) In the event a linebacker runs through the strongside gap or a defensive lineman over the strong guard slants to the inside, it becomes the responsibility of the center to pick it up. If neither occurs, he blocks the linebacker, also indicated in diagram 4-11, using the same technique as in picking up the linebacker on an odd front. In most cases the linebacker will either be blocked by the strong tackle or pursue to a point where he must be blocked past the running lane. The important thing is for the center to stay after the linebacker at any cost. The fact he has made some contact will prevent the linebacker from a clear-shot tackle.

The offset defenses such as stacks or some type of center gap, whether it is an odd or even front, are approached one way. If the defender aligns in the gap away from the play, the center disregards him and steps through the strongside gap to block the zero linebacker. Anytime the defender aligns in the strongside gap, it becomes a double-team block with the strong guard. The center and strong guard come off the line of scrimmage shoulder to shoulder with their shoulder pads under the defender's to stop his penetration and then drive him backward. It is not necessary to turn the defender, but it is important to maintain contact and keep him occupied until the play is over. (See diagram 4-12.)

⁕ Perhaps the toughest block the center must perform occurs when he steps through the strongside gap and the linebacker runs through the gap or the defensive lineman over the strong guard slants or loops to the inside. It is important in this situation to be all "eyes" to first pick up the stunt. After the location, it is important not to position-step laterally because the defender can flatten the blocker out and slide off into the ball carrier.

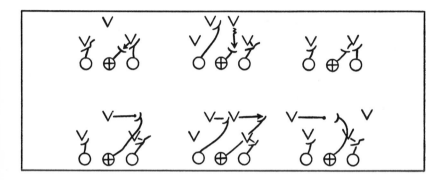

Diagram 4-11

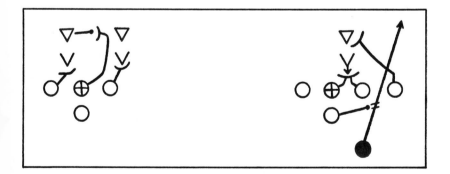

Diagram 4-12

The center must approach the defender like a cylinder, picking out the middle spot and banging his forehead through it. This will stop the defensive charge and create a stalemate. Should the blocker put his head across the front, the defender will simply push on through since the blocker does not have the bulk of his weight projected through the charger. The block must be approached at an angle to prevent this from happening. (See diagram 4-13.)

As the reader must realize, the center's block is the key one. He must be an aggressive, hard-nose lineman to execute the requirements of his position and it must be done with gusto.

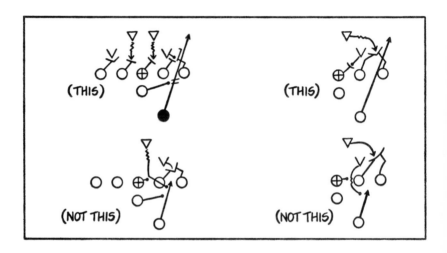

Diagram 4-13

THE STRONG GUARD

The strong guard's assignment for 71 is no. 1. The guard becomes the middle of the blocking scheme. The center, strong guard and strong tackle represent the trio of the blocking front that most affects the success of the handoff and ultimately the entire play.

Although no. 1 is the assignment, other coaching points in regard to added assignments are necessary to complete the cycle of the many defensive looks the guard may encounter. He may block no. 1 by himself, but in some cases, he will be called upon to help the center or work with the strong tackle. Since the strong guard is located between the center and strong tackle, he will be called upon to make certain calls to alert either of them about their assignment. Consequently, it is a matter of knowing whom to block in order to exercise the proper technique for success.

In the odd front, no. 1 is the linebacker playing over the strong guard. When the linebacker moves behind or shades a down lineman, the blocking scheme will change. In the even fronts, no. 1 is normally a down lineman playing over or near the strong guard. With the many possibilities of defensive looks, it becomes the responsibility of the strong guard to recognize those segments of the defense pertaining to his assignment.

The techniques of the strong guard in attacking no. 1 are similar to the center's but more involved because of the added responsibility of making "calls."

When no. 1 is a linebacker in an odd front, the guard must approach the block as though he has sole responsibility although he realizes the strong tackle will eventually help him if needed. He rolls off the line aiming his left shoulder at the defender's belt buckle. Once contact is made, the head slips by the hip with the left forearm forming the V lock. The follow-through is accomplished by snapping the head and eyes upward which drops the hips to where leg drive creates the lifting action to move the linebacker backward. In the event the linebacker slides off the block, the strong tackle is there to finish up the block. Many times I have witnessed the guard and tackle running a linebacker downfield as if he were on skates. This can occur when the linebacker plays a normal 5-2 technique.

When the 5-2 linebacker runs through the outside shoulder of the strong guard or attempts to blitz the gap between the guard and tackle, a double-team block occurs. The strong guard still approaches the linebacker the same, but the strong tackle may have to help out earlier than he does versus the normal technique of the linebacker.

Should the strong guard face the 5-2 slant defense, he will not be able to reach the linebacker. He will end up in a double-team block with his strong tackle on the defensive tackle. As he is rolling off the line of scrimmage, he will recognize this occurring on his first step. This is another important reason for the short step and all-eyes principle. As the slant occurs on his first step, he must drill his right shoulder into the slanting defensive tackle and work his hips toward the strong tackle.

When the linebacker moves behind the nose guard over the center such as in the 5-3 tandem, he is uncovered and starts the calls by the strong guard. The strong guard must call "You" in this situation. The "You" call alerts the strong tackle that he must block the defender in his inside gap by himself. (See diagram 4-14.)

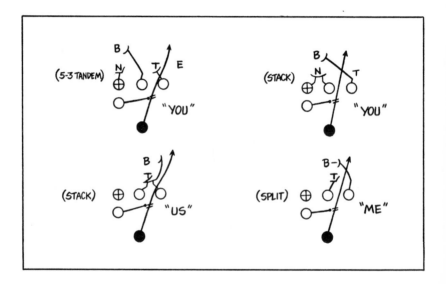

Diagram 4-14

Another situation where the "You" call can be used is versus the odd front stack defense where the nose guard and linebacker stack in the gap between the center and strong guard (diagram 4-14). The "You" call again tells the strong tackle to block by himself, but this time he will be blocking solo on the inside linebacker. It also alerts the center that the strong guard will now double-team with the center. The center and strong guard roll off the line of scrimmage, shoulder to shoulder, working to get under the shoulder pads of the nose guard. They must also get their hips together and root him out and off the line.

When the defensive tackle and linebacker stack in the gap between the strong guard and strong tackle, still another call is necessary. The strong guard either makes an "Us" call or a "Me" call. The "Us" call indicates the guard and tackle will double-team the defensive tackle to get movement off the line of scrimmage, with the strong tackle sliding off to pick up the linebacker. (See diagram 4-14.) The guard and tackle approach the block with shoulders and hips together to prevent being split by the defensive charge. After contact is made under the shoulder pads and movement starts backward, the strong tackle slides off for the linebacker and simultaneously the strong guard must fight to get his head past the outside hip and gain control of the defender. He may have to ground himself on this technique by dropping his hands downward and scrambling to get his body weight upstream.

The "Me" call, also seen in diagram 4-14, alerts the strong tackle that he is free to pick up the linebacker without the double-team. The strong guard is confident he can block the down lineman by himself. He will use the same technique as described for the center. He must attack the outside kneecap with his left shoulder. He must not position-step, such as taking a lateral step to get himself in better position to attempt the block. The strong guard must roll off the line directly toward the defender's outside knee.

The only other odd front in diagram 4-7 to cover is the 5-2 tandem. In this the defensive tackle and linebacker stack over the strong tackle. I can't imagine this ever happening because of the width of the offensive tackle. However, should it occur, the strong guard and tackle should think of double-teaming the defensive tackle such as versus the 5-2 slant. Then if the tackle steps outward, they will be in line to pick up the linebacker, who will undoubtedly blitz to the inside.

Versus the even fronts (see diagram 4-8) the strong guard is faced with a down lineman playing over him or shaded either way, the inside gap such as the 6-5 goal line and the splits which are very similar to the odd front stacks.

With the defensive down lineman playing over him, the strong guard can utilize the "Us" and "Me" call if he so desires. The "Us" call may have to be used versus the 4-3 eagle, but in either case the strong guard must first believe he can block the down lineman by himself. His approach and technique is the same as the center blocking the regular 5-2 nose guard. He must aim his left shoulder pad for the defender's outside kneecap. If the defensive lineman loops or steps to the inside the strong guard will receive help from the center as the center steps through the strongside gap. Should the defensive lineman loop to the outside, the guard probably will get help from the strong tackle. Again, it is important for the strong guard to believe he is going to block the defensive lineman by himself. See diagram 4-15 for illustrations of 4-3 defensive looping.

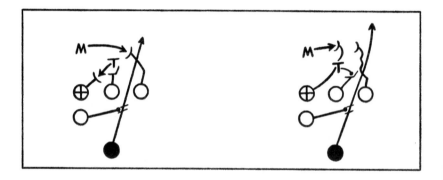

Diagram 4-15

The split defensive stunts such as split blitz and split blood can be handled the same as the 4-3 loops. (See diagram 4-8.)

The 6-5 goal-line defense presents the same situation as the nose guard aligning in the strongside gap. The center and strong guard must double-team the nose guard. Anytime a defender lines up in the strongside gap, the center and strong guard must double-team on play 71.

THE STRONG TACKLE

The strong tackle's rule for 71 is inside gap, linebacker. His assignment generally is first to a defensive lineman aligned in his inside gap and next the linebacker to his inside. The strong tackle's block must seal off the inside area to open up the running lane for the ball carrier. The ball carrier will be instructed to always stay outside the strong tackle's block. Therefore, the better the strong tackle performs, the more successful the handoff or faking action will be. It is imperative for the tackle to release off the line of scrimmage to prevent the ball carrier from running a flat course. The path of the ball carrier will naturally be at a slight angle, but if he is forced too wide, his path becomes too flat (lateral). It must be remembered we are striking almost straight ahead which has to be the best play in football. (See diagram 4-16.)

Paul Brown, the great coach of the Cleveland Browns and the Cincinnati Bengals, once said, "the best play in football is the one that hits straight ahead, and the next best is the one that hits almost straight ahead." I have never forgotten this philosophy and as I think back, the Triple may be what he had in mind. Coach Brown has probably influenced more football coaches than anyone. His successful career on every level—high school, collegiate, armed services, and professional—has put him in the number one seat among coaches. This success in every classification of football has to be considered the most remarkable record of all.

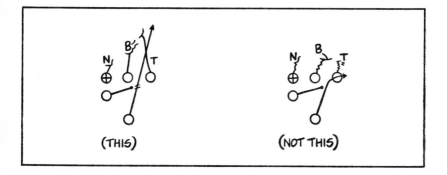

Diagram 4-16

Versus the regular odd fronts the strong tackle will have a defensive tackle playing over him or shaded slightly to his inside or outside. He must think first of rolling off the line to help on the inside linebacker. He does this by driving through the defender's inside leg. This release serves many purposes. If the defensive tackle steps to the outside, the strong tackle has a clear shot to help on the linebacker. Should the defensive tackle slam into the strong tackle to keep him off the linebacker, the strong tackle's release will enable him to turn the defender to the outside and still charge upfield. If the strong tackle steps to the inside for the linebacker, the defensive tackle can flatten out his path. This keeps the strong tackle from reaching the linebacker because his timing and release are destroyed.

Once the strong tackle clears the defensive tackle, he concentrates on helping the strong guard. Should the strong guard have the linebacker under control, the strong tackle is free to continue downfield to pick up another defender. However, if the linebacker is not properly blocked, the strong tackle must drive his left shoulder into the linebacker's near hip and close his hips to the strong guard to create a seal and double-team block.

When the defensive tackle slants to the inside, the strong tackle's release through the defender's inside leg allows perfect contact. The strong guard reads the scrapping linebacker on his release and therefore ends up in a double-team block with the strong tackle on the defensive tackle. This again is a situation when the handoff back must stay outside the strong tackle's block. His path will then pick up the linebacker and allow the quarterback to work the option on the defensive end. When the back hits inside his tackle's block, the scrape-off linebacker is free to pick up the quarterback, which frees the defensive end for the pitch. (See diagram 4-17.)

It is vitally important that the back always stay outside his tackle's block. Several coaches not understanding this principle have given up on the triple.

Once the defensive tackle aligns to the inside of the strong tackle, the stacks, splits, and 5-3 tandem become the defensive looks. This category requires the calls by the strong guard to determine the blocking assignment. Anytime the strong guard gives a "You" call, the strong tackle is alerted that he must block

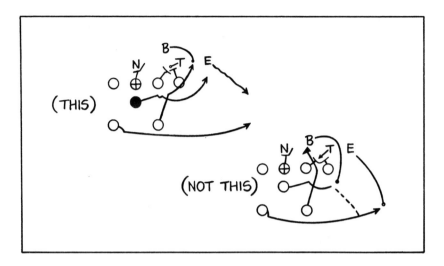

Diagram 4-17

the down lineman to the inside by himself. This results in blocking a defender in the inside gap. The defender may be charging straight ahead or playing a soft technique, reading or looping to either side. In any event, the strong tackle must assume the defensive player is charging, because this requires the toughest block. Because of the wide split of the strong tackle, the defender may have a slight edge if he comes low and hard. However, if the strong tackle maintains his space off the ball, he will be in position to stalemate and enable the back to break outside. Should the strong tackle have difficulty in stopping a hard charge, he must close his split. However, the depth the strong tackle aligns off the ball should provide enough of an edge.

The technique involved in blocking the inside gap starts with the strong tackle's stance. He may have to break his stance lower by bending the down arm or even grounding himself with a four-point stance. It must always be remembered that the shoulders drive under the opponent's. His weight must be regulated to permit the strong tackle to step toward the defender with his inside foot. He must approach the defender as a cylinder, aiming toward the center point of the cylinder.

The first step with the near foot must be short to prevent rising up and losing the battle of the shoulder pads. In aiming toward the center point, it is important the weight be released through the defender with strong, quick leg drive. Sometimes the defender will dip low with his headgear close to the ground to break through. In this case, the strong tackle must continue to get his shoulder pads underneath which may result in a "locking of the horns." The technique must be exact to stop the charge or create a stalemate. Should the defender be playing soft, the strong tackle continues the same technique and blocks the defender off the line. The strong tackle's eyes must look at the center point from the snap until contact is made. The old expression "looking the block in" gets the message across. Blanton Collier, former head coach of the Cleveland Browns, believed in the eyes so much that I sincerely believe he could write an entire book on the subject.

In some cases, the "You" call results in blocking the linebacker when the strong guard is involved in helping the center with no. 0. Again, the principle of coming off the line, not down the line, is the one to follow, for the same reason—to avoid being pushed too flat to execute the proper block. The strong tackle's approach to the linebacker employs the "hip" priority principle. We refer to this block as the optional block. The strong tackle aims his face for the numbers on the linebacker's jersey. The release is back to the principle of rolling off the up-foot, taking a short step with the back foot to prevent rising too high. As contact is made, the strong tackle "feels" the linebacker's path. If the linebacker slides outward, the strong tackle must slide his head past the linebacker's outside hip and lock the left forearm high into the V of the neck. Should the linebacker attempt to escape to the inside, the strong tackle must slide his head past the inside hip and lock his right forearm upward. If this optional blocking keeps the path of the ball carrier to the outside, it prevents the strong tackle from losing the linebacker to the inside. If the block is forced deep enough, it could possibly allow the ball carrier to break off the block. However, it may be dangerous to coach it in this particular play. It is best to instruct the ball carrier to always stay outside the offensive tackle's block.

When the strong guard gives the tackle an "Us" call, a double-team block is necessary. The double-team by guard and tackle is almost the same as by center and guard. The strong tackle has added responsibility. After movement is made, he must slide off the block and pick up the inside linebacker. As he slides off, the strong guard must slide his head to the outside to control the down lineman. The "Us" call is made versus the stack or split defense when the strong guard cannot handle the down lineman by himself. This does not occur very often, but the technique must be mastered for completeness. The down lineman cannot afford to split out too wide because of the threat of the quarterback sneak, described in a later chapter.

The double-team block must be shoulder to shoulder under the defender's shoulders. The strong guard steps with his right foot aiming his right shoulder just to the left of the defender's belt buckle. The strong tackle steps with his left foot aiming his left shoulder just to the right of the defender's belt buckle. This creates a shoulder to shoulder, shoe to shoe effect. The steps must be short to keep the hips closed for full explosion. Once the double-team starts the defender backwards, the slide begins. The strong tackle picks up the linebacker with the strong guard continuing the block on the lineman. The more movement backwards, the easier it is to block the linebacker. A good job with the double-team forces the linebacker deeper and delays his attack into the line.

Versus the splits, stacks, and especially the even fronts, the strong tackle will receive the "Me" call from the strong guard. This tells the tackle he is free to pick up the linebacker as the guard can handle the down lineman. This block occurs more than any other type in the triple's blocking scheme.

Although the guard has freed the tackle to pick up the linebacker, the strong tackle still has the responsibility of helping the strong guard if he needs it. The down lineman may loop or slant to the outside or just be too strong for the guard to handle. Whatever the case may be, the down lineman must be blocked first or the play loses all possibility of success.

We label this technique the wall-off block. In other words, we want to build a wall with our center, strong guard, and strong tackle to seal off the inside and open up what Jake Gaither (famed football coach of Florida A & M) refers to as a super highway for the ball carrier to run through. (See diagram 4-18.)

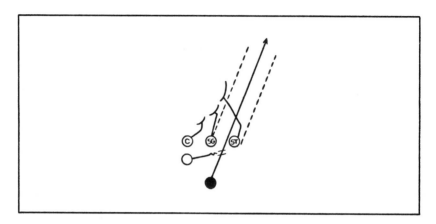

Diagram 4-18

The wall-off technique starts with the strong tackle taking a short step with his outside foot and pivoting to the inside at a twenty degree angle. Should a defender be playing over him tight, he must release upfield through the inside leg as taught versus the odd-front tackle. In either case the eyes concentrate on the outside hip of the down lineman to the inside. Should the defender's outside hip be exposed, the strong tackle must drive his inside shoulder through the hip on his path to the linebacker.

The strong tackle must look through the down lineman's hip to the linebacker. If the strong guard does not need help, the strong tackle should drive directly toward the linebacker using the "hip" priority technique.

Other things can occur in the wall-off blocking area. The defensive lineman may slant to the inside where the center and strong guard end up in a double-team; this opens the path for the strong tackle directly toward the linebacker. If the tackle looks through the defender's hip on his pivot to the inside, he will not have any difficulty in picking this up. The defensive lineman may be looping to the outside with the linebacker blitzing through the center-guard gap. In this case, the center picks up the linebacker while the strong guard and tackle end up in a double-team on the down lineman. Again, the eyes will pick up an irregularity without any difficulty. Through repetition, this will enable the proper technique to be executed.

The only possible defense that requires the center, strong guard and strong tackle each to make a single block is the true wide-six defense. The defensive guard plays over the strong guard with the linebacker aligned over the tackle. The linebacker is too wide for the tackle to consider helping the strong guard. Should the defensive guard play a regular technique, the center would not enter into a double-team with the strong guard. The center's responsibility becomes the quickside linebacker. Regardless of this assumption, the blocking scheme is not too much different from the split defense and it also should be pointed out that a true wide-six defense cannot be successful against the Cincinnati formation with the Triple - Pocket-Pass combination. The wide-six would become involved in dropping ends off the line because of the spread of the formation which in turn would dissect the interior segments of the defense.

THE QUICKSIDE GUARD

The assignment for the quick guard is No. 1. He must classify his blocks into three categories—blocking the linebacker, the down lineman, and the inside gap.

The linebacker is the most difficult block for the simple reason that the flow of the play helps the linebacker move quickly to the point of the handoff. This means the quick guard must lead the linebacker in order to have an equal opportunity. In so doing, the quick guard must step through the inside gap. This path serves a twofold purpose: it enables him to reach the crossroads (see diagram 4-19) and cut off the linebacker before he reaches the point of attack; it works magic versus the 5-2 fire or 5-2 slant (see diagram 4-7) when the nose guard slants away from the center toward the quick guard. The inside gap path for the quick guard enables him to pick up the slanting nose guard while the center picks up the linebacker. It becomes a switch in their assignments after the action starts.

The technique in blocking a running linebacker requires more effort than anything else. Arriving on the spot is the most important detail. Once the quick guard arrives, he must slide his

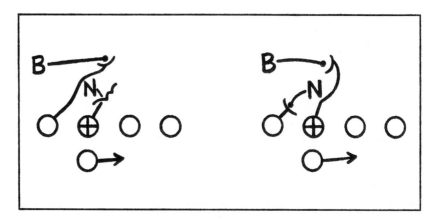

Diagram 4-19

head past the defender with the left forearm snapping up high to lock the defender's hip into the V of the neck. "Stay after, stay after" is the secret of success.

When the linebacker is lined up on the quick guard's inside shoulder such as in the split defense, the quick guard's chore becomes somewhat tougher. One consolation is the fact a defensive nose guard is not involved, so the quick guard can give his full concentration to cutting off the linebacker. Also, if the center does not become involved in the strongside blocking, he will be available to turn back and cut off the pursuit of the linebacker.

The technique in blocking the nose guard should he slant into the path of the quick guard becomes something of a collision technique. The quick guard must meet the nose guard's charge face on and then slide the head to the inside to force the nose guard to continue a circle before he is able to trail the play action.

Should a linebacker blitz, the quick guard must meet him squarely to prevent being turned inside, which would allow the linebacker to push through. A blitzing linebacker cannot be a factor if the Triple results in a handoff, but if he can break through he may catch the quarterback should he keep. Therefore, the quick guard must meet the blitz squarely and slide his head to the inside to prevent an inside breakthrough.

Blocking the inside gap becomes a cut-off block on a down lineman. It may be necessary to cut the split down. The quick guard must take a lateral step to meet the gap charge as squarely as possible, using the same technique described for the strong tackle when he blocks a gap to his inside. The difference is the lateral step the quick guard must take to get a "square-on" position prior to contact. The quick guard must not turn his shoulders toward the center. Once he does this, he loses all his power. The weight has been projected in the wrong direction and allows the defender to flatten the blocker's course, enabling an easy entry into the backfield.

The lineman playing over the quick guard as in the even defenses is sometimes referred to as a 2-technique. The 2-technique lineman can align on the quick guard's nose and on his inside shoulder. Unless the defensive lineman is involved in a slant, he will read the movement of the quick guard before he reacts to the ball. It is amazing how often this defensive lineman on the side away from the point-of-attack is involved in the tackle. With this understanding, the block becomes an important, single achievement. The quick guard must come off the line of scrimmage, attacking the defender's inside knee area. Once contact is made, the lifting action starts and simultaneously a turning of the defender away from the point-of-attack must take place to prevent the defensive lineman from taking the proper pursuit course. Much attention must be given to this block for the Triple to become a success.

THE QUICKSIDE TACKLE

The assignment for the quick tackle is no. 2. This assignment can be debated. He could be sent downfield to block on the safety. Many teams assign the offside tackle this assignment. If he is blocking downfield, he must clear inside of no. 2 on his release to prevent no. 2 from gaining a quick trail on the play. We did a study of the value of the offside tackle blocking downfield. Very seldom was he in position to help. This research involved film study of several teams. The tackle was doing an awful lot of running, but very little blocking. The argument in support of the tackle blocking downfield is that even if only one of his blocks breaks the back for the long touchdown, it is worth all the effort. However, the amount of running affects the tackle's endurance, which hurts his blocking at the point of attack when the play is directed to his side.

Another point is the fact that no. 2 in a stack or split defense is lined up in the inside gap. Clearing inside no. 2 when he is so aligned usually prevents the offensive tackle from getting downfield. The clincher in our decision was the type of personnel we would have as offensive linemen. We had made the decision to place our quickest linemen on defense. Therefore, without speed in our offensive front, we elected to have the quick tackle block no. 2.

When no. 2 plays over the quick tackle, he may slant to the inside and pursue the ball or drive through the quick tackle's outside shoulder in order to trail the deepest back. The best blocking approach in handling this type of defender is the technique of stepping with the inside foot through the inside gap. If the defender slants to the inside, the quick tackle is on top of the block perfectly. Should the defensive lineman charge to the outside, the quick tackle must pivot back, never taking his eyes off the defender and catch him coming in the back door. This second phase of the block is similar to drop-back protection technique.

Blocking a linebacker calls for the same technique the quick guard utilizes. The quick tackle must lead-step through the inside gap running to a crossroads to meet the linebacker since he will be moving quickly on the flow of the backs.

Blocking a defensive lineman in the inside gap is not as critical for the tackle as for the quick guard. The quick tackle can approach the defender as a cylinder and block through the center point. Naturally, the best block would be the cut-off technique, but unless the offensive split is cut way down it becomes a very difficult block.

In discussing the various types of blocks for each lineman for play 71, it must be remembered that the play has been illustrated running to the right from "Right" formation. Should the formation be "Left" with 71 called, consideration must be given to the descriptions; for example, if the strong tackle is called upon to block with his left shoulder for 71 in "Right" formation, he would use his right shoulder for 71 in "Left" formation.

In studying each offensive interior lineman's assignment, responsibilities, and techniques, it is important for the reader to continue to refer to diagrams 4-7 and 4-8. The many defensive looks and stunts can be found somewhere among the odd and even defensive fronts. Again I repeat, teach the player whom to block, then work on technique by repetition. If the player has too many assignments, the coach is teaching mostly assignments. Technique by repetition develops proper execution. Proper execution produces success.

THE QUARTERBACK

The quarterback's mechanics in the Triple must be perfected through complete dedication and concentration. Developing in him precision timing and confidence must be given top priority. Unless the proper method of training the quarterback is employed, the offense is going nowhere.

Before we start with the quarterback's assignment for play 71 (execute triple principle), we must understand something about man's thinking processes. Experts on the subject have proven a human being can concentrate completely on only one situation at a time. A golfer understands that when he commences thinking of the many different parts of his golf swing, he is in real trouble and will perhaps force a poor swing. He realizes that by concentrating on only one part of the swing he will experience his best swing provided he has worked out all the other parts through practice (repetition) until they are a part of his subconscious. He performs these elements by habit and concentrates on only one element to perfect the swing. The same is true in training the quarterback in handing-off, faking, passing, and operating the Triple.

The quarterback, by repetition, works into his subconscious the center-quarterback exchange and the path toward his assignment. However, the Triple has three elements—the handoff, the pitch, and the keep—to follow.

If we follow what we learned from our experts, and I thoroughly believe we should, we must teach just one part of the Triple for concentration.

Therefore, we selected the pitch phase of the Triple around which to build the play. The handoff and keep become reactions to the pitch. Therefore, we think of the Triple as a pitchout and rightly so because this is the most difficult segment to teach. A positive approach is to emphasize that the pitchout is what we are attempting most to exploit. The pitchout is the big play because the ball carrier is running down the boundary behind two downfield blockers.

In chapter three, I explained how the quarterback calls the play and gets the team out of the huddle to the line of scrimmage. Also, I explained the cadence procedure. From this point, we start play 71 in "Right" formation as the snap count is being called with the ball on its way from the center to the quarterback's hands.

As the quarterback calls the snap count, the center starts the snap and the team starts its first movement, but the quarterback turns his head toward the "read" which begins the Triple principle. The team reacts to the single sound; the quarterback must not move until the ball is firmly in his hands.

The look in the direction of the "read" starts concentration on the decision the quarterback must make for the Triple. He is thinking of the pitch unless the "read" prevents this from taking place and then the quarterback will handoff or keep by reaction, not concentration. There is a thin line between the two and it is most important the two are completely understood.

THE "READ"

The "read" is a defensive player aligned over the tackle. It can be a defensive tackle, a linebacker, or a defensive end depending upon the defense deployed versus the Cincinnati formation. Referring back to diagrams 4-7 and 4-8 (odd and even fronts), the reader can follow the "read" by each defense. Starting with the odd-front regular 5-2 defense, the "read" becomes the defensive tackle playing over the outside shoulder of the strong tackle. The defensive tackle remains the "read" in the odd defenses until he aligns inside the strong tackle such as in the odd stack and 5-3 tandem. Once the defensive tackle aligns inside the strong tackle, the defensive end becomes the "read." When the even-front regular 4-3 appears, the defensive end becomes the "read" and remains so until a linebacker aligns inside the end. The one exception to the even front is the wide-6 defense wherein the wide tackle is the "read."

After the quarterback looks directly toward the "read" on the snap, the ball will hit into his hands for him to pocket it on his belt buckle. As the ball hits the quarterback's hands, the point of the ball nearest him must be moved to that spot with the elbows close to his sides. The pocket detail is an added insurance the ball is secured by the quarterback for the operation. If the ball is not pocketed correctly, it may swing against one of the linemen or even drop out of the quarterback's hands.

Once the ball has been put into the pocket, the quarterback pivots toward his read and starts taking short steps toward the defender. It is not necessary to count the steps because the eyes looking directly toward the "read" will control body movement. How far the quarterback moves in that direction depends upon the width of the defender's alignment. The quarterback must be under control one yard from the defender's alignment or charge, to either handoff or fake the handoff to the fullback driving through. The mesh for the handoff takes place on the line somewhere from behind the outside foot of the strong guard to the inside foot of the strong tackle in their initial alignment. (See diagram 4-20.) As the quarterback moves toward the "read," he must take short steps to be under control at the mesh spot one yard from the original alignment of the "read." As he is moving toward the "read," he must point the ball directly toward the defender. The ball should be extended with the arms almost straight. The elbows must not bow outward, but remain straight in order to keep the ball level at the quarterback's belt buckle. It must be level because the fullback has the responsibility of lining up his belt buckle with the center of the ball. In order for this to take place exactly the same each time, we must decide upon the plane on which the ball will always be for the handoff.

Now, let's examine what procedure the quarterback has gone through up to the mesh spot where the handoff or fake will occur. He has barked the cadence, looked toward the "read," pocketed the ball, moved toward the "read," pointed the ball toward the "read" on a level plane, and come under control momentarily after a few short steps to the mesh spot. The process in simplest terms can be stated "look-pocket-step." This is the procedure the beginning mechanics must start for all plays. As the quarterback becomes trained in the mechanics, he will execute the look-pocket-step almost simultaneously.

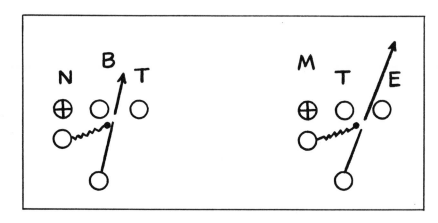

Diagram 4-20

Also, at this point, let me caution the reader that the first problem you will have in this execution is the quarterback attempting to get to the mesh spot too quickly. Speed is not necessary here if the details are followed as outlined. It becomes almost a deliberate movement to the mesh spot. Concentration is more important than speed. At the mesh spot the quarterback comes under control by slowing down his deliberate movement even more for the execution of the handoff or fake. The quarterback must not hurry, but relax and take his time as he follows the prescribed course.

The quarterback must think of executing the pitch. This is what he concentrates on from the beginning to the end. What else occurs must be a reaction. In executing the pitch he must fake the ball to the fullback, step around the defender tackling the fullback and be ready to pitch out to the tailback sprinting to the outside. To execute the proper fake to the fullback, the quarterback hooks his right elbow into the fullback's hip. As the fullback runs through the middle of the ball, he feels the elbow pressing against his side and proceeds to cover over the ball as he drives into the line and outside his strong tackle's block. As the quarterback presses his right elbow into the fullback's side, he begins breaking the ball out still on the same belt-buckle plane and back to his pocket. As the quarterback breaks the ball out, he steps around the fullback as he is tackled, ready for the pitchout technique. (See diagram 4-21.)

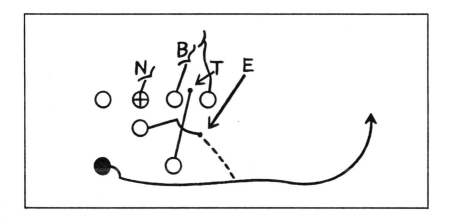

Diagram 4-21

As the quarterback moves and points the ball toward the "read," he studies the reaction of the defender. If the defender charges toward the ball, the quarterback must execute the fake handoff and be ready to pitchout as he has been thinking and concentrating. If the defender does not charge toward the ball, it becomes a reaction for the quarterback to hand off to the fullback. If this reaction occurs it is the end of the quarterback's responsibility. He can stand still and watch the play if he so desires. It is not necessary to carry out a fake beyond that point and you do not want him to because it will destroy the concentration-reaction theory and take much time to work out all the intricate details.

THE HANDOFF

The details of the handoff are very simple. The ball is already extended on the level plane. The fullback will drive through the middle of the ball making the proper pocket to receive the handoff. It is not necessary for the quarterback to find the pocket. When the fullback's belt buckle makes contact with the quarterback's hands covering the ball, the quarterback must slide his inside hand back to his pocket, keeping his outside hand on the ball until it is firmly in the fullback's pocket. Should the "read" not charge toward the ball and should the center, strong guard, and strong tackle seal off the inside, you will witness the best play in football—the one that Paul Brown said, "hits straight ahead."

When the "read" charges toward the ball, the quarterback executes the faking action, steps around the collision (tackle on fullback) and is ready for the pitch. The faking action is not really a ride and I do not believe a ride should be taught. The fake to the back lined up behind the strong guard is different from that to the fullback behind the center. In the latter, it is necessary for the quarterback to step back and pick up the fullback with the ball as he does in the inside belly for better timing and execution. However, when the quarterback is moving down the line, a ride would destroy the concentration necessary for pointing the ball toward the "read."

THE PITCHOUT

After the quarterback completes his fake to the fullback, he steps around the collision and starts the pitchout to the tailback. The pitchout must be taught in this sequence because at that moment the defensive end in an odd front or an outside linebacker in an even front may be coming hard and fast for the quarterback. The pitch is accomplished with a one-hand loft. The ball must be easily released as a basketball player executes a jump shot. It must not be pushed, shoved, or forced to the tailback. A line drive is tough to handle, but a soft floating lob can be easily handled without any miscues. The ball must be pitched to the tailback above the waist and out in front. The tailback will be sprinting toward the boundary so the quarterback must calculate the distance of the pitch by speed and width of the tailback. Making the pitchout the concentration area of the Triple will pay huge dividends and save valuable time.

THE KEEP

After the quarterback steps around the collision and prepares to execute the pitchout, he is aware if the outside defender is charging toward him. If the outside defender does not charge right away, this may delay the pitch while the quarterback continues to move laterally. If the defender decides to play the pitchout, the quarterback must react by keeping the football and turning upfield. This becomes a reaction because the concentration is on the pitchout. Should this reaction occur, the keep-running area is amazing even though the quarterback moves back away from the line of scrimmage. The fake inside whereby the "read" tackles the fullback is the greatest hold on inside pursuit I have ever witnessed. Should the outside defender play the pitchout, the quarterback has a laid-out carpet to run on for 10 to 15 yards. (See diagram 4-22.)

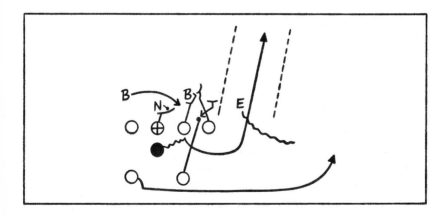

Diagram 4-22

Our quarterback at Cincinnati, Greg Cook, became the offensive leader in the nation in 1968 because of his keeps on the Triple and his great passing completions. The Triple made him a tougher quarterback and relieved the punishment a drop-back passer must sometimes endure. Because the threat of the run and pass were there, Greg was able to build up a total of 3,272 yards for one season. My quarterback coach and offensive coordinator at Cincinnati, Leeman Bennett, now backfield coach with the Detroit Lions, has to be given much credit for Greg Cook's development.

To summarize, the sequence of details involved in the quarterback's mechanics of operating the Triple can be listed—the candence-look-pocket-step-point the ball toward the "read" (reading the defender and pointing the ball toward the "read" occurs as instantaneously as recognizing hot water from cold)—if the defender does not charge toward the ball hand off to the fullback. If the "read" charges toward the ball, fake to the fullback and prepare for the pitchout—pitch to the tailback unless the outside defender plays the pitch, in which case keep and turn upfield. I must emphasize once again the importance of teaching the pitchout as the concentration area and the handoff and keep as reactions. All the details must be covered until they soak into the subconscious and become habit. It must be apparent to the reader that in making the Triple the basic running game you must be willing to spend the majority of running practice on this phase. When the details are smoothed out, the Triple comes as close to a perfect running game as can be produced in modern-day football.

THE FULLBACK

The fullback believes he is going to be the ball carrier. When he lines up his feet four yards from the line of scrimmage, his down hand will measure approximately three yards from the line. He must line up directly behind his offensive strong guard. If the fullback has an extraordinarily quick start, he should be moved one-half yard deeper so that he does not arrive at the mesh spot too soon. On the other hand, if he has an unusually slow start, he can be moved one-half yard closer to the line. Whether he moves closer or deeper, the path he runs when he is the pitch man must be taken into consideration and coordinated with the play going either quick side or strong side. In other words, the back must line up in the same position for both the handoff and the pitch, because if the play is called at the line of scrimmage the back will not be able to make the adjustment. For example, he cannot line up closer to the line for the handoff and deeper for the pitch. The feet alignment of four yards from the line is the best position unless the coach has the unusual situation of the quick or slow-starting back.

After the fullback takes his alignment, he must believe he is going to be the ball carrier. This is his concentration, with the possibility of faking the handoff a reaction.

On the snap, the fullback aims his path between the strong guard and tackle as he locates the plane of the football pointed toward the defender. As he is sprinting into this area, he lines up his belt buckle on the center point of the football. This responsibility and path coordinate the mesh for the handoff. As the fullback approaches the spot of the handoff, he must raise his inside arm high with the palm of his hand outward. The opposite hand with fingers spread is placed on the far hip. As his belt buckle meets the ball, he must clamp the ball by sliding the outside hand underneath the ball to the far point. The inside hand will come down on the ball for added protection.

Since the fullback's path is generally between the offensive guard and tackle, he is running at a slight angle. This is vital because it will enable him always to stay outside his offensive tackle's block. Sometimes it is very tempting to cut back inside, but this will soon destroy the timing and effectiveness of the entire series. The fullback should study his offensive tackle's block in order to slide outside.

I realize some coaches also teach the fullback to read the defensive tackle or "read" to help him know whether the play will be a handoff or fake. I believe this decision should be solely the responsibility of the quarterback and through the feel of mechanics, the handoff or fake will be executed. It is more important for the fullback to drive through the mesh spot correctly and study his tackle's block than to be concerned with the quarterback's "read."

Should the quarterback's "read" indicate a fake to the fullback (defender charges ball), the mechanics must adjust accordingly. As the fullback approaches the handoff spot, the quarterback will hook his elbow into the hip of the fullback. This begins the breaking action necessary to take the ball out of the fullback's pocket. The fullback reacts to this "feel" by moving his outside hand underneath until it slaps his inside elbow. This keeps the inside elbow from dipping and crowding the ball. It also serves as a tremendous fake and never have I seen it fail to draw a tackle from the charging defender. Again, the fullback must adhere to the important rule of breaking outside his offensive tackle's block. This action is also a great hold on linebackers and inside pursuers.

The fullback must be the type of runner that cannot be stopped by an arm tackle. When the blocking to the inside is strong, the fullback will be downfield with the ball before the safety realizes what happened. When a defender breaks through with just an arm or hand on the fullback, he should demonstrate enough strength and leg drive to break away. When the concentration is on the pitch, the handoff becomes a reaction and when it breaks clean, it becomes the most fascinating strike in football.

The fullback's reaction to faking must use the same drive. In the majority of cases, the fullback will be tackled by the "read," which completely takes care of the inside pursuit, but should he break on through, he should react as if he had the football.

THE TAILBACK

The tailback lines up directly behind the quick guard four yards deep. When the pitchout is made, we want our tailback to be as wide laterally as possible. On the snap, the tailback must sprint toward the sideline as though running the 100-yard dash. He should take a deep step on the snap to get more depth (five yards from the line of scrimmage) and level up and sprint directly toward the sideline. The distance between the quarterback and tailback is not important in the beginning. It is important for the tailback to get width quickly to create as much distance as possible for the defensive end or outside linebacker to cover. If the quarterback does not get the quick rush, he moves laterally and if the defender is playing the pitch, keeps and turns upfield. Then the tailback should attempt to react by keeping five yards from the quarterback and slightly behind him. (See diagram 4-23.) It is possible the quarterback may decide to pitch after he passes the line of scrimmage, so this precautionary measure requires the tailback to be in position for a legal lateral pass.

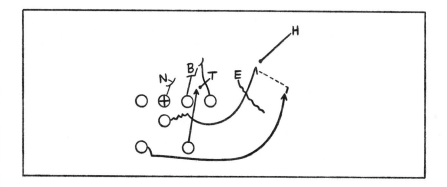

Diagram 4-23

The tailback's first responsibility is to sprint for width. If the pitchout is made early, we want our tailback to have the width necessary to put pressure on the outside corner.

After the tailback receives the pitch, he must first read the block of the wingback. If the wingback knocks his man down, the tailback must sprint outside the block, turn the corner and drive downfield. Should the secondary defender force the wingback to block him to the outside, the tailback must cut inside the block. (See diagram 4-24.)

Once he clears the block of the wingback, the tailback springs downfield behind the split end's block. He reacts the same way but can be more help to the split end by running directly toward the defensive halfback. Once the defender takes a side, the block is thrown by the split end and allows the tailback to break off the block and continue toward the goal line.

The tailback must believe the ball will be pitched to him and utilize all his speed to get outside.

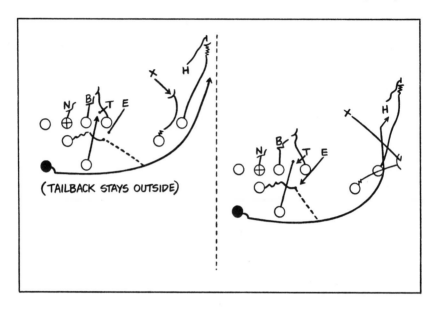

Diagram 4-24

When play 71 is operated from "Left" formation, each player has the same assignment. For simplicity sake, I have explained all the details from "Right" formation, so it is necessary for the reader to think opposite when he thinks of the play from "Left" formation. (See diagram 4-25.)

PLAY 79

Running the Triple toward the quick side and away from the formation side is numbered 79. The rule sheet for 79 is broken down by position this way:

        Split End—Hold
        Wingback—Check 26, Deep middle 1/3
        Strong Tackle—#2
        Strong Guard—#1
        Center—#0
        Quick Guard—#1

Quick Tackle—Inside gap, linebacker
Tight End—Deep 1/3
Quarterback—Execute Triple principle
Fullback—Pitchout
Tailback—Handoff

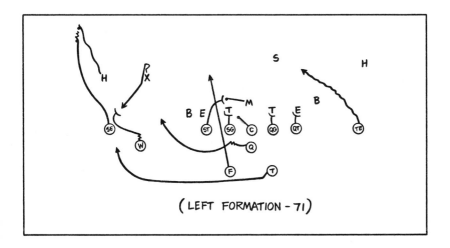

Diagram 4-25

Again for simplicity sake, let's visualize play 79 in "Left" formation (see diagram 4-26) and switch around the techniques used in play 71. For example, the wingback now has the assignment the tight end has in "Right" formation play 71. Play-action pass 26 is the opposite from play pass 24, so it is necessary for the wingback to find the throw-back area the same as the tight end does in 71 before he continues downfield into the deep middle to block.

The strong tackle and quick tackle switch assignments as do the strong guard and quick guard. The tight end now has the responsibility the split end had in 71, and since we are running into a single halfback without the safety being a factor, the wingback's short outside-1/4 block is not needed. The tailback now becomes the handoff back while the fullback races for the

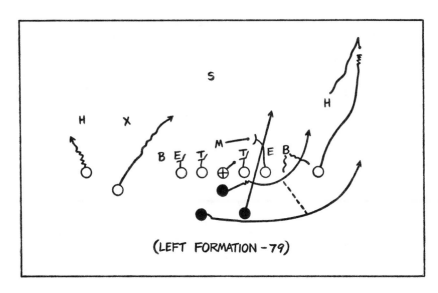

Diagram 4-26

pitchout. We allow the split end in play 79 to load off the line which ties in with a pocket pass maneuver later on.

By combining assignments and techniques, we are able to operate plays 71 and 79 from both formations "Right" and "Left" and have 12 plays that provide a complete running game. (See diagram 4-27.) The handoff, keep, and pitchout going to and

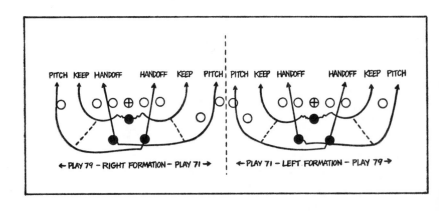

Diagram 4-27

from formation add up to six possibilities in one formation, and when the other formation is used the coach has projected the possibilities to 12.

All in all, the Triple play has more potential than any other single play. If the coach makes the Triple his basic running game, does not add too many additional plays and pays special attention to details, his running attack can succeed against any opposition. The Triple can be an equalizer when the team you are playing is superior in strength.

Five

TRIPLE OPTION

DRILLS

We must have simplicity, consistency, and ball control to develop an adequate offense. Ball control can be defined as the control of the football offensively until you either score or put your opponent in poor field position. We obtain control by repetition of execution, adhering to the details of assignments, and by giving the individual the "tools" to be an excellent football player. Therefore, it is imperative to drill the individual to precision. By repetition, we are striving for the day when the player will react involuntarily to all situations. By doing things habitually or naturally, he can start concentrating on his ultimate assignment.

For the teaching of the Triple Option, we broke our offensive squad into three groups: interior line, backs, and receivers. The coach for each group had the responsibility of teaching each individual of his group the assignment, technique, details and coaching points of each particular play. We employed certain drills for the teaching of the Triple and they were repeated time and time again.

THE INTERIOR LINE

Each drill begins with alignment and stance. This is the base to start all drills. It is important that nothing in this part of the drill be assumed; particular attention must be paid to its perfection. Although the coach always gives the stance a quick glance, he should on occasion go over the check points of the good stance to be assured that the players completely understand them. The check points of a good stance:

> Feet—Toe-instep alignment pointing straight downfield wide as shoulders; back cleats of up foot touch the ground.
>
> Ankles—Good bend, flexible.
>
> Knees—Bend forward over the toes and slightly inside the feet.
>
> Hips—Closed to insure balance.
>
> Back—Level.
>
> Head—Up only 45 degrees with neck relaxed.
>
> Eyes—Forward.
>
> Down Hand—Vertical and slightly inside of the back foot with fingers bridged.
>
> Up Arm—Cups around front of knee in ready position.

The first drill used by the line coach is the recognition one. This drill is normally done during specialty period before actual practice begins. The coach lines up his number one offensive linemen on the ball with the number two group on defense. The coach stands behind the offensive linemen and signals the defense to line up in a certain defense. He then calls a play number, walks up to the center, calls the cadence and the offensive linemen on the snap count walk through their assignments. The drill is simply for teaching assignments. The offensive linemen make any "calls" necessary and have an opportunity to check assignments against many defenses without the concern of contact. Remember, we believed in the theory that an offensive player must first know whom to block. There is no way a lineman can be aggressive if he is uncertain of his assignment. (See diagram 5-1.) The coach switches his number one and number two line around until each lineman has an opportunity to check his assignments.

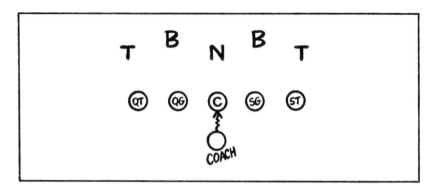

Diagram 5-1

The next drill for teaching the Triple to the lineman is called strongside technique. This involves strong guards, strong tackles, and a center on offense working against the quick side on defense. The coach sets up a defense and explains how he wants its members to react, then the offensive side will execute the Triple block. The coach stands on the side behind the defense and signals to the offense which way he wants the offense to block, whether it be 71 or 79. This gives the offense a chance to execute the proper technique toward the play called and also away. A center acts as quarterback by calling the cadence and taking the snap as the linemen fire into the defense. The purpose is to teach technique, which the coach checks much better by watching the players' eyes. Teaching the proper technique is the real challenge to any offensive coach. He can work individually on the boards, blocking on a dummy or a sled, but the job is never accomplished until it is executed in live combat. Therefore, the strongside technique is live and full speed without the aid of blocking dummies. (See diagram 5-2.)

The third drill is the same as the second, only it puts the quickside guards and tackles and a center on offense with the strongside lineman moved to defense. These live contact drills should be short with plenty of action.

The fourth drill is called blocking as a line. This puts the strong and quick side together as a unit, blocking against a live defense. It is ideal to have enough defensive linemen from the "B"

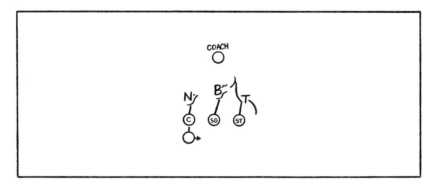

Diagram 5-2

squad in this drill so that all the offensive linemen can concentrate on offense only. (See diagram 5-3.) It is important in this drill to observe the progress made on assignment and technique.

These drills are simply for teaching the Triple, but the point must be clear that it is important for repetition to perfect the execution necessary for the Triple. The four drills can be utilized in practice daily in order to have the offensive linemen prepared for the basic running game before they join team drills.

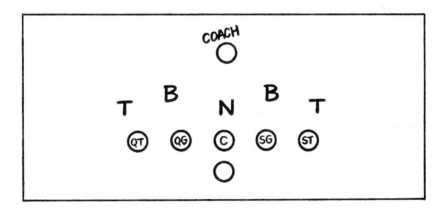

Diagram 5-3

THE OFFENSIVE BACKS

The offensive back is an intriguing figure in any attack. He must have speed, quickness and toughness, and always be in shape to sprint, sprint, sprint. He is called upon to block, carry, tackle, receive and pass, and sometimes to make the big play. Even if blocking is poor, he always tries to slash through at the point-of-attack, rip over a linebacker, twist away from an upcoming secondary defender, and outrace the pursuit for six points.

The big play may not occur many times in a season, but I firmly believe that we must practice for it anyway. We must give our offensive backs the "tools of the trade." They must believe that every time they line up and are called upon to carry, they are potential scorers.

Although we are running to score, we must face reality. The minimum distance a back should gain is four yards. Our backs were sold on this four-yard theory. It is the "bread and butter" of the offense. Consistency in perfecting this will move the ball and keep the offense in high gear.

Gaining maximum performance from our backs and adhering to the four yards or more consistency perspective is vital in our preparation. A daily ritual is necessary to check points, statistics, accomplishments, and always foster an attitude of improvement. A football player should always report to practice striving to be better when he leaves the field. Only with this attitude does he have a chance to achieve greatness.

As a prep coach in my early years of coaching, I set up some offensive backfield drills that I believed were vital to the ultimate goal. These drills were carried through my college coaching at Kentucky, Oklahoma, and Cincinnati and became known as the "Bread and Butter Drills."

As with the lineman, each drill begins with alignment and stance but ends always beyond the goal line. I studied many films to find out what happens to a ball carrier enroute to the goal line. I assure the reader once again, it is necessary to coach from films. Through intensive study of films and methods employed by other coaches, we developed our drill program.

As previously mentioned, each drill begins with alignment and stance. Without linemen properly spaced, it is sometimes difficult to line up perspective-wise. Without correct alignment, it is impossible to work on timing. To insure lining up correctly, we devised our own line of scrimmage. It was a fire hose upon which numbers painted at correct intervals designated each offensive lineman. The fire hose is easy to handle and can be rolled up after the drill and put out of the way. It is also convenient to move from spot to spot. Another "must" for alignment is lining the field with five-yard markings for at least 20 yards. This is important so that the deep backs can always judge their depth.

The stance is always given a quick glance, for many reasons. First of all, the back must have a good stance to move quickly in three directions—straight ahead, left, and right. He must do this without rising. A stance that forces a back to rise not only prevents a quick take-off but causes him to block too high.

Another necessity for each drill is to have a center for your quarterback exchange. It is senseless to expect to develop timing unless the play starts each time with a snap. When the center reports to the drill, he should have a defender opposite him on his nose, in a gap, or as a linebacker so that he may gain something also from the drill.

Diagram 5-4 reveals the area necessary for the Bread and Butter drills. The area is 20 yards in length and two-thirds of the field in width. We measured by one boundary line and two hash marks. The hose (line of scrimmage) is always placed 15 yards from the goal line. This means that in each play our ball carrier or faking back must sprint the required 15 yards to the goal.

The first drill is called "stay-in-bounds." Since the Triple is taught first as an option pitchout, it is necessary to incorporate this phase of the Triple into the first drill.

STAY-IN-BOUNDS

The "stay-in-bounds" drill illustrates the technique for the back taking the pitchout, turning the corner upfield and running down the sideline. How many times in studying films have you seen a back running down the sideline permit himself to be pushed

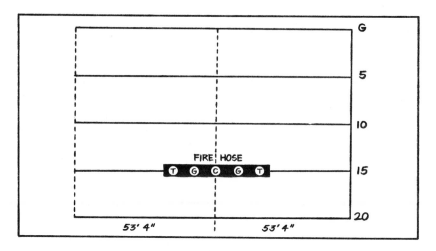

Diagram 5-4

out of bounds? This is desirable only when the situation requires stopping the clock.

The drill is set up with middle of the fire hose on a hash mark. The Triple is called in the direction of the boundary, creating a situation in which the ball carrier runs out of room and must turn upfield. As he makes the turn, three defenders with air dummies spaced three yards apart await him. Each holder greets the ball carrier with force, attempting to push him out of bounds. The dummy-holder meets the ball carrier in a football position two yards from the sideline. At this stage, the ball carrier must learn two important points. First, he squares his shoulders so that they point upfield. Secondly, he attacks the defender. He does not wait to be pushed, blocked, or tackled. To accomplish this, he drives his inside shoulder under the shoulders of the defender, turns upfield and completes the drill by scoring through a blaster machine. (See diagram 5-5.) Roger Bird, an All-American halfback at the University of Kentucky, was one of the best I have seen at staying in bounds. Many times Roger, hemmed in on the sidelines, used the stay-in-bounds technique and burst upfield for a big gain.

In this drill, the quarterback has the opportunity to read a defender, to fake the handoff, and observe another defender coming to force the pitchout. This gives the quarterback the opportunity to work on his technique of pitching out to the swinging halfback. Occasionally, the coach should have the defenders change their charge to keep the quarterback honest in his reads so he will react to the handoff and keep possibilities.

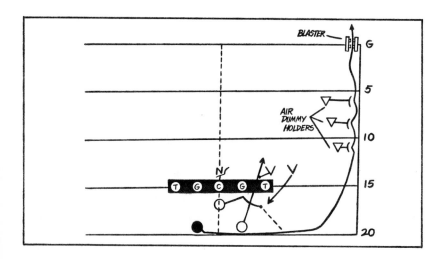

Diagram 5-5

THE GAUNTLET

The next drill is called the "gauntlet." (See diagram 5-6.) The drill is designed to execute the handoff of the Triple. The defender over the offensive tackle's position gives the quarterback the "read" to react for the handoff.

Before the drill begins, a manager slides the fire hose so the point-of-attack is in line with the gauntlet lane. At the point-of-attack spot, we place two players in a football position—shoulder to shoulder—with two air dummies straddling the lane where the ball carrier will run. Three yards from this spot, towards the goal line, three large cylinder dummies are placed horizontally one yard apart. Next in line are four players serving as the gauntlet. At the end, 15 yards from the line, is a blaster machine.

The play begins with the center-to-quarterback exchange. This is the first check point. Always emphasize a smooth snap and proper cadence and take off. The center carries out his block as the quarterback moves away from him. We stress that our quarterbacks turn the head in the direction of the "read," pocket the ball, and step. Look, pocket, step is a progressive method eventually smoothing out all these segments simultaneously.

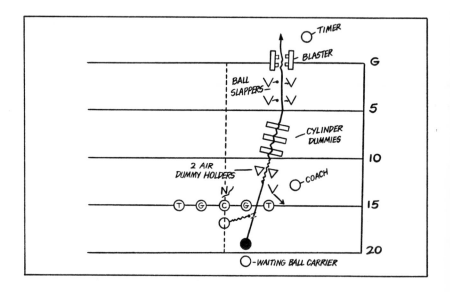

Diagram 5-6

On the snap, the back starts with real emphasis on his ball-carrying at this point. The stance is checked, the start, and the pocket the ball carrier must make for the ball, with his eyes in the direction in which he is required to run. A correct start will give him a quick burst of speed. He must not rise up; therefore, the short first step principle must be followed.

The pocket is made by raising the inside elbow with the thumb down, palm out. This prevents the elbow from sagging into the line of the handoff. The outside hand is placed in the crease of the outside hip with fingers spread.

At the handoff spot, the quarterback starts the ball in with two hands and releases the inside hand as the ball is firmly tucked away by the ball carrier. The ball carrier takes the handoff with the bottom hand sliding underneath, covering the far end while the top hand covers the "meat" of the ball. Both hands remain on the ball.

After the handoff, the back is ready to break through the two dummies. The first stage teaches the back to run where the traffic is heavy and still break between two defenders. At this point, he learns a very important lesson: if his shoulders are higher than the two dummy holders, they will close and not let him break through. He soon understands that he must run with his weight forward, body lean, and shoulders lower than the two would-be tacklers. His forehead spears through the crack as his shoulders spread the lane. His legs must pump like pistons to accomplish a smooth break. When a ball carrier does not break through smoothly, we relay the message, "You're standing at attention." This is our way of saying, "Go back and repeat."

After the breakthrough, a mental test takes place. If the carrier is only thinking of the line of scrimmage breakthrough, he will fall down as he crosses the point-of-attack. This is exactly what happens to the back in live combat. Many times he is not tackled, just bumped, yet he assumes he is being tackled and falls down. If he is mentally thinking of going all the way through the gauntlet, he will do all the things necessary to score.

To remind our backs of this necessity, we place the three cylinder dummies next in line. To get over them, he must pick up his feet. His head must come up or after the breakthrough he will look silly tripping and falling before his teammates.

After the back clears the three cylinder dummies, four teammates begin slapping the ball. The first two strike fom underneath while the next two swing their fists downward. The back must have two hands on the ball or he will fumble. In fact, we expect him to keep both hands on the ball throughout the entire drill. Only when he breaks into the open do we allow him to use one hand, and then the ball must be cradled in the outside arm.

Carrying the ball correctly is a characteristic of a great back. We taught the cross-arm method. The ball is carried across the body, scraping the rib cage. The elbow is clamped tightly over one end, and the fingers completely cover the front end. As the back runs, the ball scrapes across the body as opposed to the point pushing forward. The point pushing forward will cause a fumble when a tackler strikes the side and pins the elbow to it. The cross-arm action allows the back to run with weight forward and he must keep the other hand on the ball ready to clamp down. For this reason, we did not teach the stiff arm. We preferred that the runner keep both hands on the ball and depend upon his shoulders for warding off a would-be tackler and leg drive for acceleration.

Once the back clears the gauntlet area, he approaches the last obstacle, the blaster. The blaster is a machine with a powerful force of resistance. This simulates the goal line and completes the course the back must travel.

The time it takes the back to complete this course is clocked. If he is lined up four yards deep in the backfield, he will actually travel 19 yards. He will have to work for the yardage and do it the football way. I believe this drill gives the best time evaluation of a running back. It is amazing, but the 9.8 speedster is not always the fastest football runner. Many 10.5 sprinters can equal or better the track star.

A good back is one with time consistently around 3.2 seconds. In a five-minute period, nine to ten backs will get six or seven attempts. We posted the time on the squad bulletin board each day so that each player would be encouraged to move up higher on the list.

Occasionally, the coach should have the "read" defender charge toward the ball to keep both the quarterback and running back honest. The next defender should play pitchout, forcing the quarterback to react with the keep. When this occurs the quarterback must pick up the gauntlet at the cylinder dummies and finish the remainder of the course.

POLISH

The last and all-important drill is the polish drill. This involves the tight end, wingback, and split end with a complete backfield. The complete Triple is executed. The coach stands on the defensive side where he can watch the eyes of the quarterback and all the fundamentals of the entire backfield. The coach will control the defender's charge for the pitch, handoff, or keep. (See diagram 5-7.)

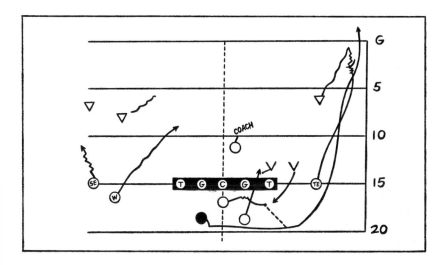

Diagram 5-7

Another "must" in all drills concerns the fumble. We expect everyone in the drill, including the dummy holders, to "dog-fight" for the ball. This attitude of reaction will carry over when the team is playing for keeps.

Game or scrimmage film should be utilized to prove to the back the value and importance of the drill work. The coach should never fail to point out to the player where one of the "tools" has enabled him to score, gain more than four yards, or make a first down. Keep score on these points and you will be amazed at the intensive progress made toward the ultimate goal.

THE RECEIVERS

The receiving coach utilizes his drill periods for the Triple similar to the interior line coach. The offensive backs have a more complex drill setup because of the many complexities involved and the "tools" needed to come up with the big play.

The receiving coach must first walk the individual receiver through the situations that may occur and explain the technique of blocking. Since the receivers will be using a roll-block technique, it is necessary to work against the large bell-bottom dummies when they go full speed.

After the individual work, the wingback and split end will go through a reading period where they must pick out the revolving of the secondary to come up with their assignments. This has been explained in the previous chapter, "Mechanics of the Triple Option," and it is just a matter of the receiver rehearsing time and again his individual responsibility until he joins the offensive backs for the polish period.

After the polish period where the backs and receivers work together, they are joined by the interior linemen for team work. The foundation is layed in the individual drills and then gradually put together for the entire structure.

Six

TRIPLE PLAY-ACTION

PASSES

It is necessary at this point to insert the Triple play-action passes before going into details on the pocket passing game. The play-action pass ties in with the Triple running game, the passes being thrown after faking the run.

Play action also differs from pocket passing in regard to the receivers: they, not the quarterback, must read the secondary. When the quarterback must fake a handoff before passing, he cannot concentrate on the secondary; therefore, he must depend upon the receiver to read the coverage and break into the open. The quarterback has the responsibility of first making the handoff fake, then setting up and finding the receiver.

Play-action passes from the Triple fit into the overall planning superbly. They supplement the running game in a way that keeps the defense from playing run when the offensive linemen and backs drop from their pre-stance into the regular three-point stance. To understand this point, the reader should refer back to the second chapter, where the Triple - Pocket-Pass combination was explained. The offensive team reports to the line of scrimmage in a pre-stance. The pocket pass threat is immediately available on the quick sound. When the pocket pass or some surprise element did not take place on the quick sound, the offense dropped into its regular stance to operate the Triple or a play-action pass. The reader can realize that if the defense was set on the quick sound to defend against the pocket pass and decided to change its thinking to stop the Triple when the offense dropped into their regular stance, it became vulnerable to the pass from play action.

The Triple play-action passes are broken down into three groups: strongside, quickside, and special passes.

STRONGSIDE PASSES

The strongside play passes indicate the play action of the Triple is toward the formation side. The quickside play passes denote the Triple action is away from formation. Special passes can be set up either way. Any number ending in 1-2-3-4 refers to strongside, while numbers ending in 9-8-7-6 designate quickside.

The assignments for the strongside protection are:

> Tight End—Check Pass 24, block downfield; stay protection—block end man; pass 24—pass pattern.
>
> Quick Tackle—#2; block tackle versus wide-6; "out" call—turn out.
>
> Quick Guard—#1; help quick side; make "out" call versus stack, 6-5.
>
> Center—#0; offside LB; help quick side; block gap away from call.
>
> Strong Guard—#1; block inside gap; make "gap" call versus gap-8.
>
> Strong Tackle—4-5-7 technique; "gap" call—block down.
>
> Wingback—Pass pattern (block for 21).
>
> Split End—Pass pattern.
>
> Quarterback—Fake handoff, drop back between strong guard and tackle (pitchout or keep for 21).
>
> Fullback—Fake handoff, pick up strongside LB; "gap" call—block first man outside strong tackle.

Tailback—Sprint laterally strongside—block end man; 21—run or pass.

Inserted in each block of Diagram 6-1 is "stay" protection. This blocking scheme is utilized on the quick side when that side is unable to handle the backside rush.

By following diagram 6-1, the reader can identify each position and pick out its blocking assignment.

TIGHT END

For passes 21-22-23, the tight end checks out the pass area for pass 24, which is the quick throwback to him. Then he is required to sprint downfield and block for the receiver if the opportunity arises.

When "stay" protection is called for, the tight end must align one yard from the quick tackle and block the end man if he rushes. The tight end uses a pocket pass technique by dropping back to the inside. (Pocket protection will be described in detail in the chapter on the Pocket Pass.)

QUICK TACKLE

The quick tackle blocks no. 2 except versus the wide-6 defensive look, when he is assigned the tackle or the second man on the line of scrimmage since no. 2 is the linebacker. For passes 21-22-23, he must utilize the pocket protection technique. For pass 24, he must block aggressively because of a quick pass by the quarterback.

An aggressive block requires the quick tackle to drive his forehead toward the belt buckle of the defender and stick with him by sliding the head past the hip on the side of the defender's charge. It does not matter which direction he is blocked. The important thing is to keep the defender's hands down and stick with him the required four seconds. Effort in staying with the block is most important.

When "stay" protection is called for, the quick tackle blocks the first defender inside the defensive end man whether the former be a lineman or linebacker.

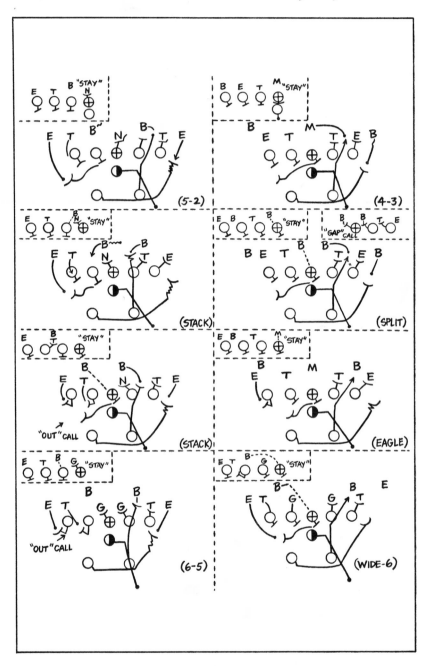

Diagram 6-1

THE QUICK GUARD

The quick guard is responsible for #1. When #1 does not rush, such as the linebacker in a 5-2 defense, the guard checks back to help the quick side. His next most important responsibility becomes the defensive end rushing outside the quick tackle's block.

The quick guard must use a pocket protection technique on the linebacker if he rushes or the defensive end if the linebacker does not rush. In blocking a linebacker running through, it is necessary for the quick guard to get back two quick steps in order to step around the center's block should the linebacker blitz through on the strong side. When the linebacker blitzes, it is important to step to the inside to give the linebacker only one path through which to rush. The quick guard is now in position to meet the rusher with the proper technique. Once the quick guard is assured the linebacker is not rushing, he must pivot his left shoulder around, move to a position outside the quick tackle and be ready to meet the outside rusher if one is coming. If an outside rusher is not coming, the quick guard is free to help out in the area.

Versus the 3-technique stack and the 6-5 defenses, the quick guard must make an "out" call. This call turns the quick tackle out on the next man and allows the quick guard to block his man. This recognition is picked up because of the center's rule against those defensive looks. The quick guard uses the pocket protection technique when blocking out. The "out" call is the true pocket protection (55) block for the guard and tackle. These techniques will be explained in more detail in the chapter on the Pocket Pass.

When "stay" protection is called, the quick guard stays with no. 1. This is his sole responsibility.

For pass 24, the quick guard must block aggressively on no. 1. Should he be a linebacker, the quick guard must remember that if he makes contact, he must stay with his block or be called for being downfield during a pass which is a penalty of 15 yards. Once he loses contact, he must drop to his knees and remain there until the pass is completed. If the linebacker is too far away to reach, the quick guard must force into either the center's or quick tackle's block. Because of the nature of the pass it is important to stay low and be aggressive to prevent the defensive front from reading pass.

THE CENTER

The center first blocks no. 0. If no one is lined up in the zero area, he is responsible for the offside linebacker. In either case, if the man does not rush it is the center's responsibility to pick up the defensive end rushing outside the quick tackle. Should the defensive end not be rushing, the center is free to back up the quick guard and tackle should they need help.

When the center has a linebacker or the defensive end to block, he must use the pocket protection technique. When no. 0 is the nose guard, he uses an aggressive technique.

When a defender aligns in either gap or both gaps, the center is only responsible for the gap away from the call. This also must be an aggressive block.

When pass 24 is called, the center must remember that any block he makes must be aggressive. Should the linebacker be too far back, the center should fire into the quick guard's block since the strong guard has the faking action of the fullback to help his block.

THE STRONG GUARD

The strong guard has the assignment to block no. 1. When a defender aligns in the inside gap, the strong guard must block him. When defenders align in the inside and outside gaps, he must call "gap" and block the defender to his inside. "Gap" alerts the strong tackle to block the gap defender to his inside.

The technique for the stong guard must be an aggressive block in all cases. Since the faking action takes place on his side of the line, he must perform the aggressive technique in order to conform to the play action. The purpose is to present the defense with a running play look and read. This keeps the defense playing for the Triple run rather than rushing the passer.

The strong guard must aim his forehead toward the defender's belt buckle and use the hip priority technique by taking the defender any way he wants to go. It is important to meet the defender squarely to prevent losing him to either side. Once contact is made, the blocker must stick with his assignment for the required four seconds. The faking action will help the blocker accomplish this important task.

Should the defender be a linebacker, the strong guard must remember that if he loses contact while pushing the linebacker downfield, he must drop to his knees to prevent being called for blocking downfield during a forward pass.

Blocking the defender in the inside gap has been previously described.

THE STRONG TACKLE

The strong tackle receives his assignment from the defensive-technique numbering system. He is responsible for any defender on the line of scrimmage in a 4-5-7 technique—this means any defender lined up on his nose or outside shoulder to the next defender outside. He blocks aggressively, the same as the strong guard, in the order 4-5-7 defensive technique.

When the strong guard calls "gap," the tackle blocks down on the first defender on the line to his inside. He is not responsible for a linebacker since this is the fullback's assignment.

THE WINGBACK AND SPLIT END

The wingback and split end are in all pass patterns except for 21, when the wingback is expected to block in front of the tailback on or behind the line of scrimmage in the event a defender comes up in the outside fourth of the field to press the runner. Pass 21 is an option run or pass by the tailback on the pitch out.

THE QUARTERBACK

The quarterback's duties will be detailed in the explanation of each pass.

THE FULLBACK

The fullback is responsible for making a good fake of receiving the handoff and then picking up the linebacker to his side and sprinting directly through the defender for the success of the play action. He should aim directly toward his strong guard, making the proper pocket so the ball can be put on his belt buckle, with his eyes on the linebacker. As the ball is pulled out, he slaps his elbow and drives toward the linebacker.

When a "gap" call is made, he is responsible to block the next man outside the strong tackle. This means his path will have to change slightly to the outside in order to veer outside to pick up the next defender. The quarterback is responsible for putting the ball or hand into the pocket before he sets up to pass.

When 21 is called, the fullback should run the path he normally runs for the Triple. Since the quarterback will continue to option the defensive end, this path will aid the quarterback's true action in the Triple.

THE TAILBACK

The tailback sprints laterally until he is beyond where the fullback was originally lined up. Once he reaches this point, he must drive directly toward the defensive end man. His blocking technique from this point on is not to drive into the defender, but to get a yard or so away because the quarterback is setting up to his inside. From this moment on, it is necessary to use the drop-back pocket protection technique which will be explained in detail in the chapter on the Pocket Pass.

When pass 21 is called, the tailback must run it exactly like the Triple. If the ball is pitched to him, he has the option of running or passing.

Again, for simplicity sake, I will explain each play-action pass in "Right" formation. The reader must keep in mind each play or pass can and will be duplicated in "Left" formation.

PASS 22

Twenty-two is the basic strongside pass. (See diagrams 6-2 and 6-3.) The split end is the primary receiver. While the quarterback is faking the play action and setting up, the split end must read the defensive "X" man (or inside safety) to determine whether to run a post or circle route. In diagram 6-2, the "X" man comes upfield into the short outside. This tells the split end to break into a post route. Should the "X" man drop back into the deep one-third, the split end should break into a circle route as indicated in diagram 6-3.

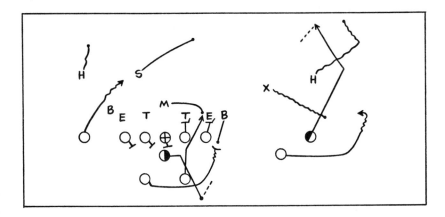

Diagram 6-2

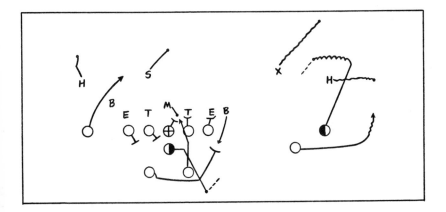

Diagram 6-3

The split end releases off the line of scrimmage, aiming two yards outside the defensive halfback. On his seventh step (outside foot) he breaks into a post or circle route. Upon his release, he must begin to read the "X" man in order to be ready for the break. This read enables the receiver to be in the open area for the reception and takes advantage of the vulnerable area of the defense.

The quarterback has the responsibility of carrying out the proper faking action and setting up to find his split end.

On the snap count, the quarterback's eyes snap around to pick up the fullback's belt buckle and he moves laterally along the line to prepare for the fake. He should meet the fullback behind his strong guard or slightly wider, depending on the fullback's path to accomplish his blocking assignment. This movement is just a few short steps; therefore, it is important to use the eyes, which will control all the movement necessary for the quarterback to arrive at the correct spot. Since the quarterback will be setting up after the fake, I believe in using a hand fake. The quarterback holds the ball in both hands until the fullback reaches the mesh spot. At this moment, the quarterback puts his left hand into the fullback's pocket, holding the ball in his right hand against his stomach. As the fullback runs through the quarterback's hand and slaps his elbow, the quarterback turns his shoulders away from the line of scrimmage, snapping his left hand back to the ball. The turning of the shoulders hides the ball as the quarterback retreats to a spot (seven steps) behind his strong tackle. As the quarterback is sprinting back to his setup spot, his head must be turned back toward the line of scrimmage in order to pick up the split end. Once the quarterback sets up, he is ready to throw the post or circle route to the split end.

The wingback drives laterally five yards outside the original alignment of the split end and then turns upfield under control. The wingback is an outlet in the event both secondary men on his side back up as shown in diagram 6-4. Then he is open in the short outside one-fourth. The quarterback is aware of this possibility and can throw to his outlet if he so desires. The wingback must be certain his inside shoulder is back out of the way for a pass. If it is thrown behind him, it is difficult to make the catch without the chest facing the passer.

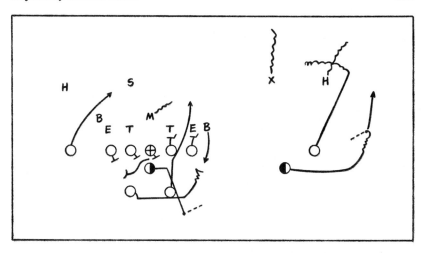

Diagram 6-4

PASS 23

Twenty-three is a pass designed to hit the wingback in a vulnerable area between the linebacker and the "X" man (inside safety) toward the formation side. (See diagram 6-5.)

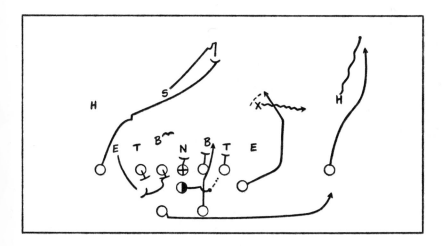

Diagram 6-5

The wingback lines up in the closed position (one yard from the strong tackle and one yard off the line of scrimmage) and releases across the face of the end man for three steps. He should execute a flat release and on the third step, turn upfield for four steps. On the upfield fourth step, he must break slightly to the inside looking over his inside shoulder for the pass. Should the "X" man play him man for man, the wingback must make a move to the outside on his upfield push before breaking back to the inside. (See diagram 6-6.)

The split end has the responsibility of pushing deep to force one of the defenders to cover the deep one-third of the field.

The tight end clears his throwback area and must be prepared to block in front of the wingback after the reception.

The tailback sprints toward the sideline to keep the end man concentrating on the option and out of the quick-throwing lane.

Twenty-three is a quick pass for the quarterback. He fakes the ball this time to the fullback because time will not allow a hand fake. The ball must go into the fullback's pocket with both hands remaining on it. The back of his right hand must press against the fullback's belt buckle. The ball is then pulled out as the fullback makes the fake by slapping his right hand against the left elbow and drives hard toward the linebacker. The quarterback then raises up and hits the wingback in the vulnerable area.

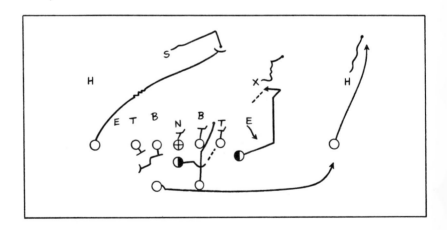

Diagram 6-6

On the snap count the quarterback snaps his head around to pick up the fullback's pocket for full concentration on the faking action. The faking action plus aggressive blocking by the strong-side linemen gets the credit for the success of this quick pass.

PASS 24

The quick throwback pass is 24. (See diagram 6-7.) This pass is very similar to 23 except the quarterback passes to the tight end on the quick side.

The tight end has been dragging through the quick throwback area when 71 is called to check out the open spot. When 24 is called, the play is live and the tight end can expect the pass to come his way after the quarterback fakes to the fullback.

The wingback drives downfield to block in front of the tight end and the reception, while the split end runs a quick sideline to occupy the coverage in his area.

Since the pass is thrown back to the quick side, it is necessary for the quick guard and tackle to execute aggressive blocks as indicated in the assignment.

Pass 24 is clever strategy. It is especially effective late in the third and fourth quarters. It was a lifesaver for us many times at Cincinnati. The linebackers must run to pursue the Triple and in

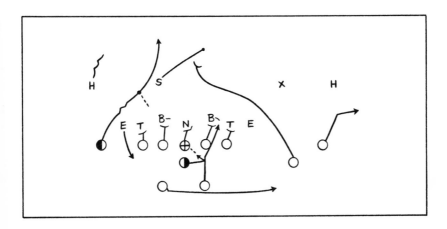

Diagram 6-7

doing so eventually became vulnerable to the quick throwback area. If this pass can be saved until late in the game, it will be good for three or four completions of 15 to 20 yards each. For this reason, the tight end must always check out this area when 71 is called.

PASS 21 OPTION

Twenty-one option can be an exciting play. (See diagram 6-8.) If the coach is blessed with a halfback who can throw the long pass on the run, this run-pass option can add tremendously to the Triple attack.

The quarterback fakes the handoff exactly as in the Triple, steps around the fake to the fullback and prepares to pitch to the tailback. Should the defender play the pitch, the quarterback must keep and turn upfield. When the ball is pitched, the tailback puts it under his arm, intending to pass only if the split end is wide open.

The split end sprints off the line, forcing the defensive halfback deep as he does in the Triple. As the split end comes under control, he faces the defender as if to block him. Once the

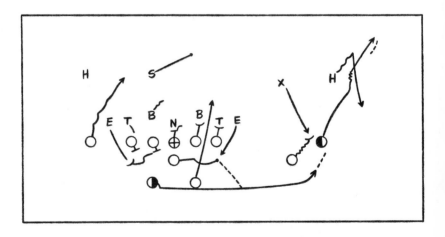

Diagram 6-8

defender breaks upfield, the split end drives for the flag looking over his outside shoulder for the pass.

The wingback blocks as in the Triple, but must not cross the line of scrimmage because of the passing possibility.

The tight end carries out his assignment as in 71.

Some have suggested the 21 option pass should be made a part of the Triple, which would change the name to Quadruple, but I believe the additional wrinkle might destroy the Triple's timing and undermine its aggressiveness. Therefore, I recommend the 21 option be a separate play.

QUICKSIDE PASSES

Passes 28, 27, and 26 fall under quickside Triple play-action passes. These passes complement the Triple handoff, keep and pitch when executed to the side away from the formation.

The protection assignment rules for the quick side are:

Tight End—Pass Pattern.

Quick Tackle—4-5-7 technique; "gap" call—block down.

Quick Guard—#1; block inside gap; make "gap" call versus gap-8.

Center—#0; off LB; help strongside; block gap away from call.

Strong Guard—#1; help strongside; make "out" call versus stack, 6-5.

Strong Tackle—#2; block tackle versus wide-6; "out" call—turn out.

Wingback—Check pass 26, block downfield; stay protection—block end man; pass 26—pass pattern.

Split End—Push downfield.

Quarterback—Fake handoff, drop back between guard and tackle (pitch out or keep for 29).

Fullback—Sprint laterally quickside—block end man; 29—run or pass.

Tailback—Fake handoff, pick up quickside LB; "gap" call—block 1st man outside quick tackle.

As far as assignments, technique, and execution are concerned, the reader will realize the same is true on quickside as on strongside. For example, the tight end and wingback switch assignments as do the quick tackle and strong tackle, the quick guard and strong guard, and the tailback and fullback. The quarterback and center reverse their techniques to the quick side while the split end pushes downfield to entertain the coverage in that area.

PASS 28

Pass 28 is like 22 except the wingback is not involved in the quickside pattern. The quarterback has only the tight end with which to work. The tight end reads the safety. Should the safety cover deep (see diagram 6-9), the tight end runs a circle pattern breaking into the seam between linebackers. Should the safety come up inside (see diagram 6-10) to support the defensive front, the tight end breaks for the post. The quarterback needs only to set up after the fake to the tailback and find his tight end. The tight end reads the secondary for the proper route to execute.

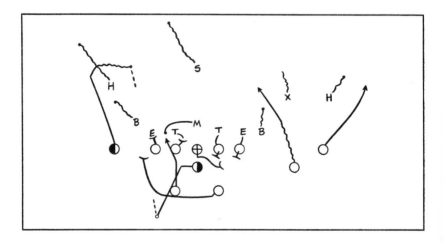

Diagram 6-9

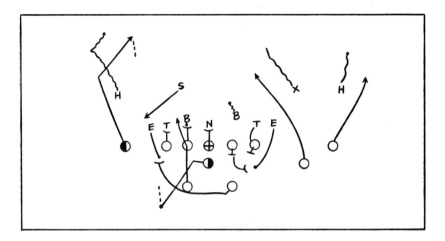

Diagram 6-10

PASS 27

Pass 27 is the opposite of 23. (See diagram 6-11.) The tight end's route is slightly different from the wingback's since it is not necessary for the tight end to take a flat release. He can push directly downfield four or five steps and then pop into the open area to the inside.

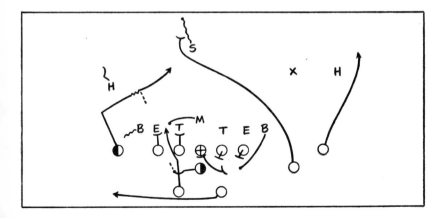

Diagram 6-11

PASS 26

Pass 26 is the mirror image of 24. The wingback must check out this area when Triple 79 is being executed the same as the tight end does for 71. The wingback finds the vulnerable area when 26 is called. (See diagram 6-12.) This is the quick throwback pass that becomes so important late in a contest. It must be remembered that both sides of the line execute aggressive blocks.

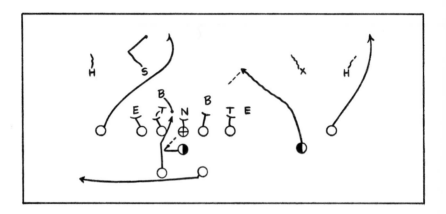

Diagram 6-12

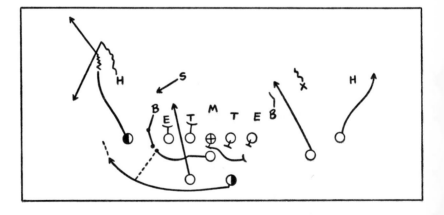

Diagram 6-13

PASS 29 OPTION

The 29 option run or pass is much like 21 option pass. (See diagram 6-13.) The fullback now becomes the passer should the quarterback pitch. The quarterback must remember it is not mandatory to pitch. If the reaction to keep presents itself, the quarterback must do so. Also, the fullback must be instructed to run first and pass only if the tight end has broken toward the deep corner clear as a whistle.

Seven

THE TRIPLE

SUPPLEMENT

Many coaches have asked me, "Well, what else do you run with the Triple? What other plays can you run? Can I have both the two-back and the three-back Triple?"

These questions are difficult to answer because what one coach can accomplish with his squad may be entirely different from what another coach can. So much depends on the personnel, the coach's knowledge of a particular offense, and the ability to teach on the field.

I recommend the coach select either the two-back or three-back Triple and build around that decision. I chose the two-back Triple because it coordinated with my pocket-passing game to give us the best combination in football. The great Bud Wilkinson, the former University of Oklahoma coach, referred to it as the best of both worlds. However, Darrell Royal of Texas has proven the three-back Triple within his Wishbone-T formation can be devastating.

Whichever way the decision goes (2-back or 3-back), one strong point must be understood. The most important thing is to establish the Triple Option. If the Triple is perfected, very little else is needed to complement this explosive series. It then becomes a matter of personnel. How can you utilize a great back, or a blocker, or a good receiver, or what does your quarterback do best—run, sprint out, pocket pass, etc? These are questions the coach must ask himself. In other words, each coach should add to the Triple what best "fits" his particular situation.

ADDITIONS TO THE CINCINNATI TRIPLE

To this point I have only dealt with the Triple (71-79). It has been carefully analyzed step by step. Some football teachers believe in giving their squad members several plays at one time and then working out the details. Others believe in taking one play at a time until it is executed to their expectations and then move on to another play. The Triple is even more detailed since the play itself requires a step-by-step approach. Therefore, the theory of one play at a time must be the procedure once the Triple itself has been perfected.

The first play added was the *quarterback sneak*. This play is a must in any offense. It is still one of the best short-yardage plays in football. With only inches to go for a first down or a score, the quarterback sneak is the number one security play. Since only the quarterback will handle the ball, the percentages are very high for success.

The sneak also helps the Triple. The wide splits of the offensive guards create a middle opening that is unbelievable when defenders on the line shade the offensive guards' outside shoulders. Diagram 7-1 illustrates the sneak versus several defenses. The blocking scheme is simply wedge blocking. Versus an odd front, the center becomes the apex with the guards and tackles stepping inside to form the wedge. Versus an even front, the quick guard became the apex. The apex blocker blocks straight ahead with the outside blockers stepping to the inside with their inside shoulder under the armpit of the player to their inside. The important message to get across in this block is quickness and movement. Also, the battle of the shoulder pads must again be emphasized. The blocker must have his shoulder pads under the opponent's. In our goal-line attack (inside the five-yard line), we sold our offensive linemen on crossing the goal line with their shoulder pads. They believed if they did this, we would score.

Since we numbered all our plays, the quarterback sneak was

called 15. The quarterback's technique involved a timer's step. If he hit the wedge too quickly, he would become bottled up in the traffic. A timer's step is necessary to allow the wedge to form and start movement. Also, the wedge creates a crack somewhere in the area and if the quarterback times his dash, he will see the opening and be able to drive through for the important yardage.

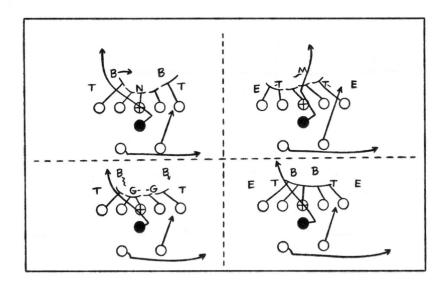

Diagram 7-1

We employed two "silent" automatics involving the quarter-back sneak. First, when a defensive lineman jumped offside, it was automatic for the center to snap the ball to the quarterback. Anytime the defense wanted to give us five yards without the loss of a down, I was glad to be on the receiving end of the gift. This requires the quarterback always to have his hands in place when he is under the center. It is a good habit for the quarterback to get into anyway because a lot of fingers have been jammed when the center snapped the ball on the wrong cadence. On the automatic snap the quarterback's reflexes should be trained so he squirts right through, because he just might score.

The second "silent" automatic involved an alertness by the

quarterback in noticing the interior defensive linemen resting when the quarterback put his hands under the center. If the quarterback felt the defense was not ready prior to the start of the cadence, he pressed the center's crotch with the back of his top hand with three quick movements. This alerted the center to snap the ball and fire out to block. The quarterback moved quickly, paralyzing the defense and also our other squad members.

QUICK COUNTER

The *quick counter* is the next play that was added at Cincinnati. (See diagram 7-2.) It was apparent the linebackers and the inside pursuit really moved quickly to the side where the Triple was being executed. The quick counter became an inside handoff back inside the linebackers and the inside pursuit. The play was numbered 74 when called toward formation with the fullback the ball carrier and 76 when called away from formation with the tailback as the carrier.

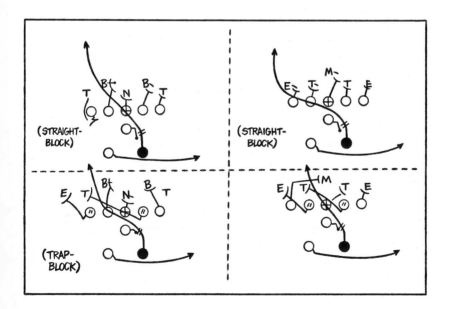

Diagram 7-2

Straight blocking was used except in some games when we decided to trap (indicated also in Diagram 7-2).

The ball carrier started directly toward his offensive guard and then cut back over the center. The back read the center's block on the nose guard for his break (the opposite guard if the defense was even). One of the key blocks when using straight blocking was the opposite tackle's. For example, in play 74, the quick tackle had the key block. If the defender's assignment was playing loose, the quick tackle would get into pocket pass protection to draw the defender upfield to create a wide offside running lane. However, if the defender was playing tight, the quick tackle had to come off the line and block aggressively, staying with his block. Somehow, when the latter developed, the ball carrier would break all the way behind the tackle's block.

The quick counter is a simple play but very effective versus a quick-pursuing defensive front. It fit into our scheme very easily because it did not involve a great deal of added teaching and time.

OPTIONS 71-79

The third play added to the Triple attack was out of necessity. There comes a time when you will want to run just the pitch or keep phase of the Triple. It might be because of some problem occurring on the handoff, or to take advantage of a weak defender, or to exploit a good outside runner. It could be just a need to get outside on a particular down and distance situation. Whatever the reason, it is important to be able to call just the pitch-keep option.

Our reason for adding it was to get outside versus the soft corner defenses presented to us because of our pocket-passing game. The defenses gave us the handoff more than the pitch-keep because of its alignment. Therefore, to mix up our attack and have a way to get a running play on the corner, we devised *Options 71 and 79*. The word *Option* before either 71 or 79 served to communicate the play.

Straight blocking was used by our interior linemen with one change of technique. This involved the offensive tackle on the side the play was called. When Option 71 is called, the strong tackle's assignment is no. 2. His release should be through the outside leg of the defender. If the defender was stepping to the outside, the strong tackle would be in position to block him. Should the defender slant inside, he would be picked up by the fullback and possibly the strong guard. This would free the strong tackle to pick up the linebacker. The strong tackle was not concerned with losing the defender to the inside although he would, in most cases, get a piece of the charger. This technique required the fullback to drive inside the strong tackle's block and pick up either a slanting down lineman or an inside linebacker.

This is just the opposite of the true Triple, where it is necessary for the running back to stay outside the tackle's block. The quarterback stayed off the line slightly, faked the ball to the handoff back, stepped around and executed the pitch-keep phase of the Triple. The difference for the quarterback is to take the ball to the fullback because the fullback's path will be decided by the charge of the defense, although it will be very close to the Triple path. (See diagram 7-3.)

Options 71 and 79, like the quarterback sneak and the quick counter, were easy to install because of their simplicity and similarity to the Triple attack. It also filled the void when it became necessary to direct the attack to the corners.

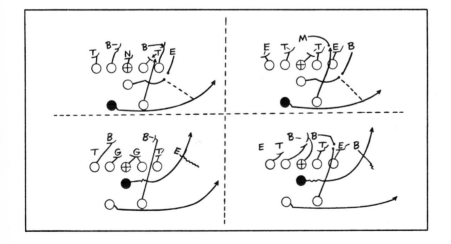

Diagram 7-3

REVERSE AT 9

The fourth play added was called *Reverse at 9.* This was really a special play and was used sparingly during the season. Very little time was spent on its execution and in most cases it was only reviewed on Thursday prior to a Saturday game. The reverse took advantage of the speed of our split receiver, Jimmy O'Brien, and was only used as a surprise element. It was never called more than twice in any one game and therefore was given only slight preparation.

The play started exactly like Option 71, the quarterback faking to the fullback and stepping around to pitch to the tailback. On the snap, the split end came back off the line to be in line for the pitch to the tailback behind our strong tackle. It was necessary for the split end and wingback to line up closer to the interior. After the split end received the pitch, it was important to gain depth to set up the peel back blocks of the quick guard and tackle. (See diagram 7-4.)

The blocking scheme for the reverse was simple since it required again the straight blocking setup. The quick guard and tackle were taught to block their assignments aggressively and lose them to the inside to set up the second block (peel block). The center, strong guard, and strong tackle released downfield after their blocks to pick up a different-colored jersey.

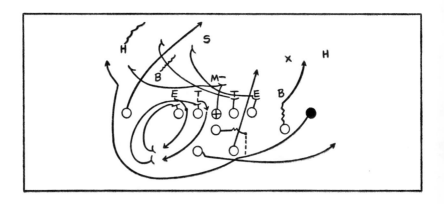

Diagram 7-4

The reader should not consider the reverse a bread and butter play because it is a "hit or miss" proposition. It can be a big gainer in certain situations and will help to slow down the offside pursuit.

COUNTER OPTION

The fifth and sixth, and final, plays added to the Triple attack were those in the counter option series. The counter option series involved a handoff and a pitch-keep option. The handoff away from formation was numbered *36* while the counter pitch-keep option to the quick side was numbered *39*.

In diagram 7-5, handoff 36 is illustrated. This is a counter to the Triple handoff which precedes the counter pitch-keep option. The quarterback fakes a handoff to the fullback, pivots and hands off to the tailback. The tailback must take a timer's step toward the formation to allow the play to unfold. As he is receiving the ball, he must read the guard's block. The quick tackle has blocked down while the quick guard drop-steps and waits for the defender playing over the quick tackle to commit. Should the defender charge upfield, the quick guard blocks out while the tailback

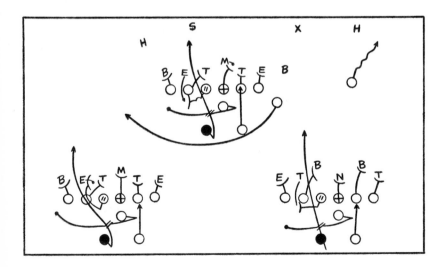

Diagram 7-5

breaks inside the block. However, should the defender step to the inside with the quick tackle, the guard must "log" him to the inside and allow the tailback to break outside his block. The tight end turns out on the end man to make this possible. On the snap the wingback sprints around the corner to set up the option.

The reader will notice in diagrams 7-5 and 7-6 the wingback and tight end are closed for this series. This is vital for the play's success and since the wingback and tight end vary their alignment in other situations, this will not be picked up by the defense. Diagram 7-6 illustrates play 39 (option). The blocking is the same as 36 except for the tight end, who releases inside the end man for the defensive halfback. The block on the defensive back is the same technique used in 79.

The quarterback now fakes a handoff to the fullback, pivots, fakes the counter handoff to the tailback, and proceeds to option the end man. The quarterback must execute a time-consuming fake to the tailback breaking between guard and tackle to allow the smoke to clear for the option. Should the defender playing over the quick tackle charge, the quarterback should dart inside him following the tailback.

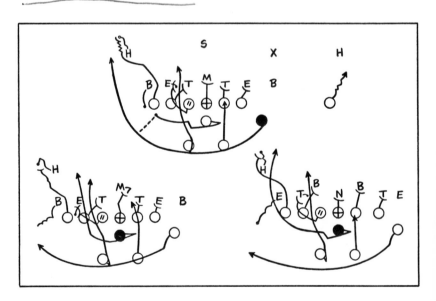

Diagram 7-6

The counter handoff and option can be executed to the formation side, but the tight end must become the pitch man. (See diagram 7-7.)

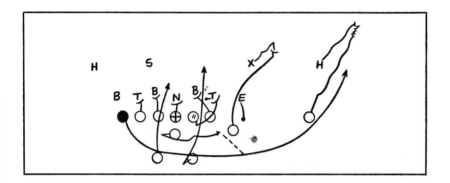

Diagram 7-7

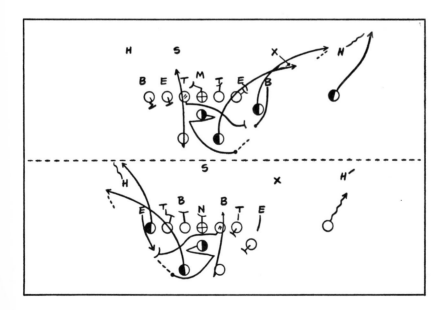

Diagram 7-8

The counter option has been used several different ways by other teams and can become a successful part of the overall offensive planning. It was used sparingly at Cincinnati mainly because of our excellent passing game. We became concerned that we might be attempting too much and so we limited our attack in favor of precision of execution.

WAGGLE PASS

The only play-action pass that was added to the two-back Cincinnati formation was a play action from the counter option called waggle at 1 and waggle at 9.

The action has a tremendous hold on the middle segment of the defense and allows a three-out pattern to strongside or a two-out pattern away from formation. (See diagram 7-8.)

Eight

THE POCKET PASS—
PROTECTION AND
TECHNIQUES

There are not enough superlatives to explain the excitement of the passing game. If you know what you are doing with the forward pass, you can pick defenses apart many ways. You may be down three or more touchdowns and come back to win. It is exciting football, the fans and players love it and it is fascinating to coach. The football in the air can be an equalizer when the people you are playing are strong physically. The combination of the pocket pass and the Triple Option with its play-action passes is the best of both worlds.

It is imperative to have an adequate passing game in today's football—one that is sound, simple and consistent. The coach who fails to exploit the passing game is undermining his career. This does not mean his teams should line up and just throw the football. The team should be able to run and pass, thus developing a complete offense. The defensive coach must plan to stop both the run and the pass. If he fails to prepare for both, he will be looking for another job. Therefore, it is only common sense for the offensive coach to prepare both run and pass. Each defense has a weakness and unless the offensive coach has a complete offense, he will not be able to take advantage of these weaknesses.

Our pocket passing game was broken down into three parts at Cincinnati: the protection and coverage, the receivers, and the quarterback. After the techniques were mastered, the plan (Pass 55) was put into operation as explained in chapter two. After the plan came the different combinations, the draws and the screens.

PROTECTION AND COVERAGE

Our protection rules are very simple. We picked out a man and stayed with him. This allowed our backs to be in maximum protection if needed. Because our formation spread the defense from sideline to sideline and we snapped the ball from an up position on the quick sound, the defense was forced to line up quickly and show any tendencies early, which also aided our linemen in recognizing their assignments. As in the Triple, the assignments are simple, thus allowing more time to work on technique. By recognition, we know whom to block; therefore, we can spend more time in teaching how to block. As I have often repeated, this is the secret to offensive success.

The protection rules are:

> Quick Tackle—second man on line of scrimmage
> Quick Guard—first man on line of scrimmage
> Center—No. 0, quickside LB (coaching point: men in both
>   gaps—block quickside)
> Strong Guard—first man on line of scrimmage
> Strong Tackle—second man on line of scrimmage
> Fullback—strong LB, end man, flare
> Tailback—quick LB, flare (coaching point: versus wide-6
>   block end man)

By examining diagram 8-1, the reader can follow the blocks through each defensive alignment.

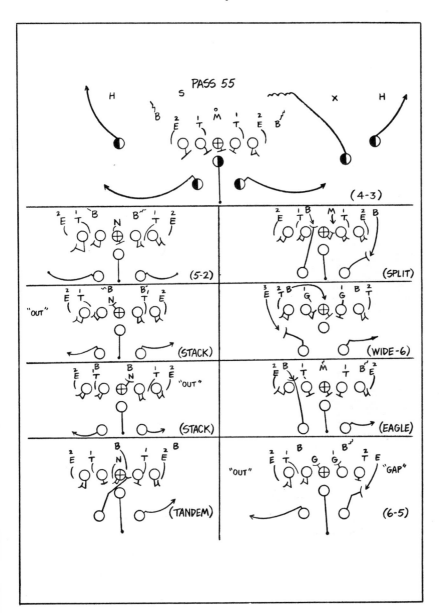

Diagram 8-1

THE QUICK TACKLE

The quick tackle's rule is the second man on the line of scrimmage. This means he must count the number of defenders on the quick side of the line of scrimmage (excluding linebackers) and block the second man. In some difficult recognition situations, the quick guard can help the tackle with an "out" call. This eliminates any doubt because the quick tackle simply picks up the defender on the line to his outside. The guard is in position to recognize the immediate tendencies.

THE QUICK GUARD

The quick guard's assignment is the first man on the line of scrimmage. He has one call to make involving Pass 55. Whenever a defender aligns in the gap between the quick guard and the center, the quick guard must call "out." This aids the quick tackle in recognizing his assignment and keeps the blocking scheme consistent. The defender in the gap will be blocked by the center.

THE CENTER

The center's rule is no. 0 (of our defensive numbering system), quickside linebacker. The center must first check for no. 0. If he is not there, the center picks up the quickside linebacker. The center is also responsible to block a defender in either gap. For communication purposes, the center made an "over" call to his guard to indicate he, the center, would handle the gap block. This allowed the guard to ignore the gap defender as the first man on the line of scrimmage and, to insure that his tackle also understood, the guard made an "out" call. When the defense places a defender in each gap, the center's responsibility is to block the quickside gap. The center called "loaded" which informed the quick guard to call "out" for his tackle and the strong guard to call "gap" for the strong tackle.

THE STRONG GUARD

The strong guard's assignment is identical to the quick guard's except for the "loaded" call, when he is required to block the defender in his inside gap. This required a "gap" call to alert the strong tackle.

THE STRONG TACKLE

The strong tackle's assignment is the same as the quick tackle's with the exception of the "gap" call, when the tackle is required to block the next man on the line from the gap defender inside the strong guard.

THE FULLBACK

The fullback's assignment is strong linebacker, end man, flare. The fullback first checks the strong linebacker. If the linebacker does not blitz, the fullback pivots to the outside to pick up the end man. If the end man is blocked or is not rushing, the fullback flares to his side as a potential receiver.

THE TAILBACK

The tailback's assignment is similar to the fullback's except that he is working on the quick side. Also, the tailback very seldom has an end man to block. Only against a wide-6 defense or the eight-man front does this occur.

EIGHT-MAN FRONT

The only defense that presents a problem is the eight-man front if the entire eight defenders rush. The quick side is handled but an extra man will come from the outside on the strong side. Therefore, we made the quarterback responsible for him. As long as the quarterback understands this, he can get the ball away on time. The eight-man front cannot be effective versus the Cincinnati passing game.

TECHNIQUE—INTERIOR LINEMEN

The technique for the interior linemen is the same for each.

Therefore, it is convenient for the line coach to spend a lot of time on individual performance. Ray Callahan, now Head Coach at Cincinnati, and Ralph Staub, now offensive line coach at Ohio State, did a superb job with our offensive linemen at Cincinnati in teaching valuable techniques.

Our blocking technique for the linemen starts with a football "ready" position—our pre-stance. Since the linemen will be in the up position for this particular block at least 80% of the time, they will have the most advantageous position for executing the pocket protection block. Another important factor involving alignment is the distance of 11 inches off the line. The distance factor is important because assuming the defender will shed the blocker in a given amount of time, the longer the block can be delayed the better. Most defensive linemen will line up as tight on the line of scrimmage as possible when rushing the passer. The blocker must realize he is fighting for fractions of seconds, so every conceivable method must be utilized in delaying the rusher. Although I would prefer to talk to the blocker in terms of six seconds, four seconds is a more realistic effort and will get the job accomplished.

The lineman breaks from the huddle, concentrating on his assignment. This does not mean he should glare at his opponent, tipping his hand; by looking straight ahead, using peripheral vision to pick out his man, he can begin concentration. As he gets into an up position with the proper spacing and alignment, he must be ready to execute the proper technique immediately, since it is smart to snap the ball on the quick sound for the pocket pass a high percentage of the time.

On the snap the blocker must snap his eyes toward his assignment, start his feet moving inside his shoes, staying in the football position and moving immediately to an inside-out position on the defender. The blocker should move backwards, taking only quick, short steps up to a depth of two yards. The inside-out position allows the rusher only one path to the passer. It is important not to set square on the rusher, which allows the defender to rush to either side. The inside-out position must be so designed that the only path is to the blocker's outside. If the rusher elects to rush to the inside, he will have to run directly through the blocker. Many offensive linemen interpret the inside-out position as a pivot with their shoulders parallel to the sideline. This is the worst position he can be in because the rusher will tear through the blocker's head to the passer without any difficulty. The blocker has lost all his power in this position and opened the gate to the quarterback. The inside-out position should be approximately a 20-25 degree angle. The position should be so designed that the bulk of the blocker's weight will be able to strike through the bulk of the weight of the rusher.

As the rusher approaches, the blocker must be set in a football position with his hips closed, shoulder pads lower than his opponent's, toes digging in in order to release his entire weight through the defender. The blocker must not attack until the defender is close enough—until he sees the "whites of his eyes." In other words, let the rusher come to you; do not go after him. When the rusher is close enough, the blocker must drive his forehead and shoulders through the middle of the defender. The target is generally around the defender's numbers. The "hit" should come from the hips, rolling off the balls of the feet as the hips tuck to release the maximum impact. This is a blow which comes all the way from the toes.

Two things can happen when the "hit" occurs; the rusher will be stopped momentarily or he will stick to the block and continue his rush to the outside. Should the block stop the rusher, the blocker wants to re-set by regaining the football-ready position and continue to "pop" the rusher as many times as possible. This phase is the ricochet segment of pocket protection. Once the rusher sticks to the block and continues his outside rush, whether it is the first strike or a later one, the blocker should "ride" with the block, allowing the defender's momentum to carry the blocker to the outside of the pocket.

It is important for the blocker to stay on his feet throughout the block with one exception. Should the blocker start to lose his man, he must go into a scramble technique. The scramble technique requires the blocker to get on all fours keeping pressure and staying after the ankles of the defender. The scramble is the last resort but can be effective because it forces the rusher to keep his hands down to play off the blocker. With the defender's hands down, the quarterback can see his receivers.

Another important detail of the blocker's technique is the use of his hands and elbows. The rules will not permit the offensive blocker to use his hands on the defender, but the rules will permit the rusher to use his hands on the blocker as long as it is not interpreted as defensive holding. For this reason, it is necessary for the blocker to be able to use his hands and elbows within the limit of the rules to counter the rusher's special privilege. The blocker must keep his elbows in tight to his waist with his hands fisted and together to help ward off the use of the opponent's hands. The defender will attempt to pull the shoulder pads or jersey, or use several other methods which allow him to escape from the block and have a clear shot at the quarterback. The blocker's fists in front become a part of his blocking surface to keep the defender's hands from grabbing the jersey. The elbows in tight are in a position to knock the defender's hand off the jersey or shoulder pad. As with the back in the Triple Option drills, it is important to give the blocker all "the tools of the trade" within the rules as he strives for perfection in his technique.

In certain situations, the offensive lineman will be assigned to block a defender rushing through his inside gap. The block should be handled as a gap block, explained earlier, in the running game. It must be an aggressive block whereby the blocker attacks the defender, scrambling with him for the required four seconds.

TECHNIQUE–BACKS

Technique for the fullback and tailback is different since most of their blocking is executed on blitzing linebackers. The backs must always look and step in the direction of the assigned linebacker. If the linebacker is coming, we taught our backs to continue on and run through the linebacker and take him out the same way he came. The important phase of this block is to meet the linebacker at the line of scrimmage before he builds up momentum. When the linebacker does not blitz, the back checks for an end rushing. If none is coming, the back can flare to his side to reduce the coverage to a one-on-one situation.

Should an outside rush come from a linebacker or end, the back should move for width and use the same inside-out technique as the linemen.

COVERAGE

The coverage phase of the protection is most important. It must begin as the ball leaves the quarterback's hand. The team sprints into position to prevent a runback should an interception occur. The backs are responsible for making the call. They call the direction "right-right-right" or "left-left-left" or "middle-middle-middle." This call gives the team direction and allows the players to release their blocks and sprint laterally (pursuit course) in the direction called.

The coverage is not a negative approach. The reader must realize there will be interceptions, so it is important to be prepared to switch to defense. We never want an interception, but if it occurs, we definitely do not want to give up a long run or a score. Because of the nature of our passing game (deep passes), the defenders have a low percentage of interceptions. The short, flat passing game is vulnerable to the interception which many times results in a score.

THE RECEIVERS

The receiving department is an exciting part of the passing game. Being better than an average receiver requires a lot of work. It means run, run, run, and catch, catch, catch. It was always stimulating to walk onto the practice field to observe the receivers running and catching.

Our patterns were simple, which allowed the necessary time to work on the little things: stance, release, steps, looking the ball into the hands, putting the ball away properly, and knowing what to do after the catch. Running with the ball after the catch is just as important as starting the release. Speed is vital in this area because many yards can be added to the reception if the receiver has this God-given ability. Also, a lot of time was spent on reading the different coverages. As I mentioned, we believed in the long pass. Therefore, our receivers had to run a lot of deep routes. It is difficult for a defensive halfback to cover the deep territory of a football field. In basketball, a defensive player can stay between his man and the basket, but in football he must cover from the goalpost to the flag. (See diagram 8-2.)

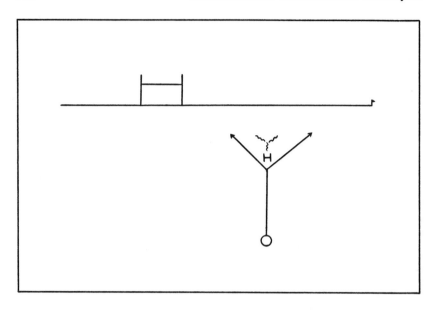

Diagram 8-2

RECEIVER'S STANCE

The first area of instruction is the stance. As mentioned earlier, we flipped our formation. This meant a receiver might be called upon to line up on either side of the field. When the receiver is lined up on the left side, he should be instructed to utilize a left-handed stance (left foot back) and when on the right side, a right-handed stance (right foot back). The outside foot back is necessary to coordinate the step-count method. The receivers learned to step-count their various routes. This allowed us always to get the distance we were working for and to compensate for the differences in speed among the receiving corps. The receiving coach should spend 5 minutes every day just emphasizing the step-count without a ball being thrown. We believed in adapting our receivers to the quarterback and not the quarterback to the receivers. If the burden is on the quarterback to throw to the different speeds of the receivers, he will soon become discouraged.

The stance for the receiver is always a down position. Even though the guards, tackles, and backs were in a two-point stance in the pre-stance and quick cadence situation, the receivers were down ready to explode off the line. I believe this is the position from which the receiver can get his best release and if he is being held up on the line of scrimmage, the down position gives him more opportunities of escape. His stance should be the same as the down-position taught for the other positions, with the weight forward ready to roll off the line of scrimmage.

RELEASE

The release is a four-step burst of accelerated speed. It occurs when the ball moves. By this, I mean the receiver must look in toward the ball and move on the snap. Since he is set wide and sometimes unable to hear the cadence because of the crowd noise, it is wise to teach movement of the ball. This does not mean the receiver should turn his head completely to the inside, but just enough to pick up movement of the ball. It also aids the receiver in hearing the "check-with-me" automatics. The head should be pointed downfield with just a slight turn for vision. This small detail will prevent the needless penalty of offsides by a wide receiver.

The weight is on the up foot and the down hand as the receiver rolls off the up foot for the explosion of the release. This release cannot be an easing-off start. It must be a quick start with all the explosion possible.

We taught both an inside and an outside release. The outside release was the first taught a receiver working versus a single defender. Assuming the defender is playing head on or on the outside shoulder anywhere from four to eight yards deep, the release should be aimed two yards outside the defender. This type of outside release immediately widens the secondary coverage and forces the defensive back to turn his feet outward and work harder for width and depth. The defensive back is concerned with the cushion he must play a receiver. The outside release really makes him run to get this cushion. If the defender fails to respect the outside release, he is immediately out of position to play an outside cut.

The first of the four steps of the release is the outside foot touching the ground as the receiver rolls off the up (inside) foot.

The steps are counted one-two-three-four with the fourth being the inside foot touching the ground. The outside release with the quick burst of speed should force any defender to get on his "horse" and run deep.

THE CONTROLLED AREA

The next three steps are called the controlled area. This does not mean the receiver actually slows down, but he should sink his hips lower which will decrease his speed slightly to enable him to make a cut on his seventh step (outside foot). Mentally and physically, the receiver must be able to cut off the seventh step for the three basic routes. Being under control will permit the receiver to cut into the next phase of his route, called the "stick." The "stick" is also a three-step move. It is toward the inside and will force the feet of the defensive back to the inside and put him out of position for the basic cuts. The "stick" area is a slowing-down zone for the receiver to make his ultimate cut to conclude the pass pattern he was instructed to execute.

THE STICK

The "stick" serves another important role; it is the "sign" for the quarterback to start his throwing action. In most cases, the ball will be released while the receiver is in the "stick," without looking for the ball. As he turns, the ball should be on its way. By this method, the defender is being forced into a position from which he cannot return in time to compete for the ball in the air. It is a simple matter of logic since the receiver knows when and where the ball will be thrown and the defender must play for the deep pass since the "stick" encourages this.

After the "stick," came one of the three basic cuts—the post, circle, or bend. (See diagram 8-3.) We ran only three basic routes plus a broken route that can occur from two of the basic three. Our philosophy in the passing game was to work with only a few routes, but to execute them with perfection. This allowed us to spend time on protection and study different ways to get the ball to the receivers.

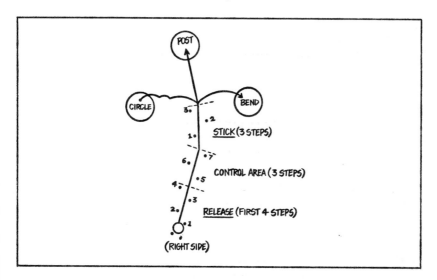

Diagram 8-3

THE POST ROUTE

The first route is called the post. (See diagram 8-4.) This is a deep route. We believed we had to establish the deep route for our other routes to stand up. On the release, the receiver must sprint off the line, aiming two yards outside the defensive halfback. The first four steps must be at top speed. The next three steps are slightly controlled. On the seventh step, the cut is made, at a slight angle toward the goalpost. The outside release forces the defender to turn his feet to the outside. On the seventh step, the break back to the inside will turn the defender's feet back to the inside which results in a race between the receiver and the defensive halfback. If the ball is perfectly thrown, it is very likely the receiver will catch it in full stride with the possibility of scoring. If the ball is overthrown (the quarterback is trained never to underthrow), the pass is not a failure because of the precarious position in which the defensive halfback finds himself. The defender now becomes very concerned over the deep route.

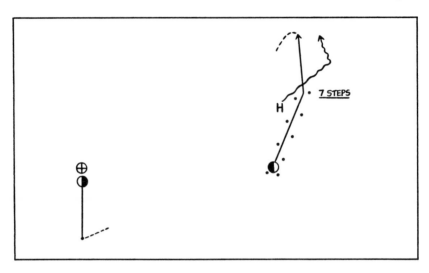

Diagram 8-4

THE CIRCLE ROUTE

The second basic route is the circle. (See diagram 8-5.) It starts exactly like the post route—seven steps (outside release) and break. On the break, the receiver takes three steps toward the post, then turns inside looking for the ball. The three steps toward the post serve as the "stick," giving the illusion the receiver is running the post route. This forces the defender first to turn his feet outside, then back to the inside on the "stick" phase. The "stick" starts the defensive halfback running to cover deep as the receiver turns to catch the ball between linebackers. If the ball does not come immediately to the receiver, he should continue to slide inside away from the defensive halfback and between the linebackers. The pass will be caught anywhere from 14 to 18 yards deep, depending on the path of the circle by the receiver. Therefore, the reader can realize my emphasis of throwing deep patterns. This is deeper than the linebackers can cover and at the same time pushes the deep secondary deeper because of the possibility of the long pass. This can only be accomplished, however, with your quarterback setting up at seven steps.

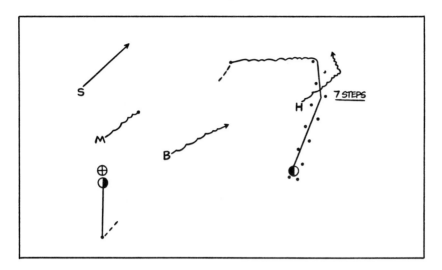

Diagram 8-5

THE BEND ROUTE

The third route is the bend. (See diagram 8-6.) The bend starts exactly like the post and circle routes—seven steps (outside release) and cut. On the cut, the receiver takes three steps and breaks to the outside. The three steps serve as the "stick" to give the defensive back the illusion that the receiver is running the post or circle route. As the receiver is going into the "stick," the quarterback starts his throwing action and will drive the football to the outside, belt-buckle height. As the receiver completes the "stick," he should snap his head around and attempt to see the ball coming out of the quarterback's hand. He must forget about steps at this point and break toward the ball. The "stick" will enable the receiver to catch the ball and run after the catch. Like the circle route, the bend is 14 to 18 yards deep. The route will turn the defensive halfback's feet outward, inward, and outward on the final move. Each time the defender must move deeper and farther from the receiver. The step-count method arranges exactly what the coach is working toward in the passing game.

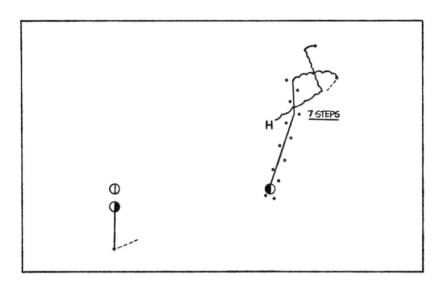

Diagram 8-6

THE BROKEN ROUTE

The broken route is not a called route, but can develop when either the circle or bend route is called. This route is the most exciting pass route in football. The deep route is very successful when the defensive back makes a mistake and the receiver runs by him for the long bomb. This is exactly what occurs in the broken route.

The quarterback calls either the circle or bend route in the huddle. The receiver explodes off the line of scrimmage with every intention of running the called route. However, if as he reaches the controlled area of his route (after the release and prior to the "stick") the defensive back stops or squares up to play the circle or bend, the receiver signals the quarterback just prior to his "stick" and runs by the defensive back. The signal may be anything the quarterback can recognize. This allows the quarterback to hold up on his throwing action, re-set and unload the long bomb. (See diagram 8-7.)

The receiver can break by on either side of the defensive back, but once he passes the defender, he must look over his inside

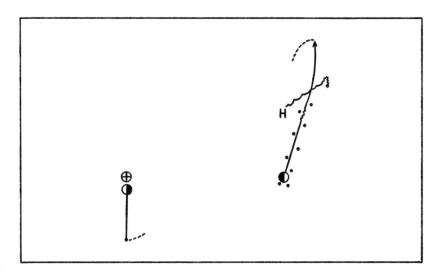

Diagram 8-7

shoulder for the football. The deep route is there when the defensive back makes the big mistake.

We discovered the broken route many seasons ago. In studying films of different receivers, my associates and I discovered that many times the receiver would have been open deep if he had run by the defender. Most defensive backs perform an adequate job of reading the receiver's various pass cuts. When a deep route is called, he is on top of it as well as on the sideline and inside routes. He is vulnerable to the deep route when he reads or senses a shorter break. When he reads a shorter route he will slow down or stop and square up on the receiver. Invariably, his weight will shift to his heels and at this very moment, if the receiver will sprint deep, the defender is caught flat-footed and completely out of position to obey the one principle his coach has always insisted upon, "never get beat deep." I have noticed many times that a receiver was a step beyond the defensive back only to turn in or out to complete his pass pattern because this was the route called and he had been instructed to run it without alternative.

Back through the years, I can remember some big wins as a result of the broken route. Two of my quarterbacks at Highland

High School, Billy Straub and Roger Walz, were experts in picking up the deep pass for big plays. Roger Walz picked up his split end, Bobby Steinhauser, for six points to break open a 1960 semi-final state playoff game and put us into the finals (which we won). Rick Norton and Rick Kester at the University of Kentucky teamed up for three touchdowns against the number one team in the nation in 1964 (Mississippi) for a big victory. In recent years, Greg Cook and Jimmy O'Brien at Cincinnati connected on nine broken route scores in 1968, three being the difference between victory and defeat.

The called deep route (the post) and the broken route will force the defensive secondary to play cautiously deep, allowing the receivers to catch a lot of bend and circle routes. Because of the depth of the bend and circle routes, a completion means a first down. In the three-down zone, the percentage requirements are only one out of three. With execution of details, this can easily become a reality. My quarterbacks always connected on over 50 percent of their passes. This is the reason, in this type of passing game, we were always near the top nationally.

The three basic routes (plus the broken route) must be adhered to in every detail. The step-counting will aid greatly in establishing the perfected passing game. It aids tremendously in coordinating the timing between passer and receiver. It is important to adapt the receiver to the passer. Should the receiver be too fast or too slow, it is a simple matter of adjusting his steps by increasing or decreasing the number of steps to time out with the passer. Also, the coach is greatly benefitted by the step-count method in studying films. He cannot always see the lines on the football field, but he can always count the receiver's steps to see if he cut too soon or too late. I can recall times when a coach jumped the quarterback for delivering the ball too late or too soon when it was the receiver's cut that was mistimed. The passing game is a game of timing.

Not enough can be said for the outside release. It increases the width of the passing lanes and forces the defensive back to cover more area. As the defender works to gain a cushion on the receiver, he becomes vulnerable at the breaking point and allows the receiver to get him head on whereby the "stick" turns the defender away from the final cut.

RECEPTION CONCENTRATION

Most receivers get to the point where they do not have to concentrate on the steps but perform them subconsciously. This is important because it is necessary to teach concentration on looking the ball completely into the hands. Upon the final step of the "stick," the receiver should be instructed to snap his head around and concentrate on seeing the ball released from the quarterback's hand. The concentration should be narrowed to the tapered end of the ball and look it all the way into the hands. The eyes again play an important role in football in seeing the ball from the quarterback's hand to the receiver's hands.

Jim Kelly, great receiver for Sid Gilman's Cincinnati teams of the late '40s, was my receiving coach at Cincinnati. Jim taught the best hand position for receptions. When the pass was chest-high or higher, the palms were turned outward with the thumbs crossed. When the pass was thrown below the chest, the palms were outward with the little fingers crossed. At all times the elbows were close to the sides and the "give" that Jim taught reminded me of a suction. The ball did not escape if it was on target.

Once the football is secure in the hands of the receiver, he must put it away under his outside arm. Once the ball is stored away, the receiver uses the same technique of carrying it as the back. The next factor is speed. The receiver should make every effort to score, increasing his reception yardage.

INSIDE RELEASE

Although the inside release is considered an advance stage of the passing game, it is necessary to teach because of certain coverages. When a defender plays outside the wide receiver either forcing the receiver back to the inside or preventing an outside release, it is necessary to execute the inside release. The inside release is also a good change of pace versus a single defender. When the man-for-man defender becomes accustomed to turning his feet outside for the outside release, the inside release completely baffles him.

Diagram 8-8 illustrates the inside release for a circle route versus outside coverage. The inside release is a six-step maneuver before the receiver breaks into the "stick" followed by the basic cut. The "stick" is now an outside move.

It is possible to work out any type of pass cut imaginable by applying the step-count formula, along with the three-step "stick." It must be remembered that with the receiver's outside foot back any inside pattern will work on even numbers while the outside releases require an odd number of steps.

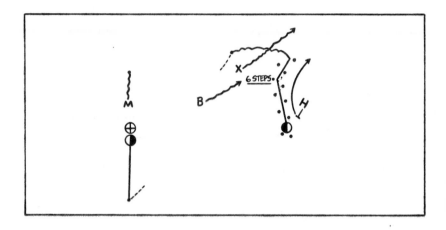

Diagram 8-8

THE QUARTERBACK

Training the quarterback for the pocket pass is the most challenging and stimulating experience the offensive coach will ever encounter. This position requires the most dedication, concentration, and off-season work.

Because I was a quarterback throughout high school and college, I had more than just an interest in this position. The many details and techniques always intrigued me to the fullest. Throughout my coaching career, I always studied the many different ways of training the quarterback until I came upon a program I believed in and one which realized success year after year. In fact, beginning with my first quarterback, Bubby Bardill at tiny Wartburg Central High, Tennessee, in 1951, through Greg

Cook at the University of Cincinnati in 1968, each of my quarterbacks was awarded All-Conference, All-State, or All-American honors. In between Bubby and Greg were George Perry at Spring City, Tennessee; Billy Straub, Richie Emmons and Roger Walz at Highlands High School (Ft. Thomas, Ky.); Jerry Wollum and Rick Norton at Kentucky; and Bobby Warmack at Oklahoma.

There have been several great quarterback coaches and in each case, they always adhered to the belief that it is necessary for the quarterback to work four seasons out of the year to become better than an average passer. If the quarterback fails to do this, the coach will only have an average offense.

Also, each quarterback teacher will agree there must be some raw talent to begin with before he can develop the quarterback into a better-than-average performer.

The art of passing is a gift, but before the quarterback can become a real winner for his team, he must be willing to work year round to perfect the passing touch. The fall season is the time for execution. The winter, spring and summer seasons are the periods for developing the technique.

The quarterback will be asked to report to pre-season practice in top physical condition, the same as each member of the squad. In addition, he will be asked to report with his throwing arm in top physical condition. If the coach has to wait half the season for the quarterback to regain his normal throwing action, the complete passing game never can be developed. The time to start the training program for developing the quarterback is during the spring practice. Should the coach be in a situation where he is not allowed to conduct spring drills, he has a real handicap. This means he must use part of his fall pre-season practice for the beginning training program and then request the quarterback to work the rest of the year on his own to develop the various techniques of the passing art. In intercollegiate football, it is important that the quarterback be so thoroughly instructed in the passing program that he can work on his own in the off-seasons (winter and summer). The NCAA restrictions will not allow the coach to be present during these off-season drills.

Nine

THE POCKET PASS

PLAN OF ACTION

The coach must cover in spring practice protection and coverage, techniques for receivers, and a training program for his quarterbacks.

In the fall it is time to develop the passing plan (55) as described in chapter two.

If the reader incorporates the passing plan illustrated in chapter two, the protection rules and routes for receivers, he has a built-in game plan for each week along with his Triple Option and its play-action passes.

When 55 is called, the tight end runs a bend route, the split end runs a post route, the wingback takes an inside release for a circle route working on the inside linebackers, and the fullback and tailback flare to their respective sides if their assignment does not rush.

This gives the quarterback a plan to start with and by picking out his "keys" and "reads," he can pass to the receiver with the least coverage.

After the quarterback establishes 55, he can call any of the three basic routes for his wide receivers. Whichever he calls (post, circle, bend) will be executed by both the tight end and the split end. In diagram 9-1 the quarterback has called Right (formation)

55 bend. By keying the safety, he knows before the snap he will be throwing to his tight end. Therefore, it is a simple matter of setting up and drilling the ball toward the bend target.

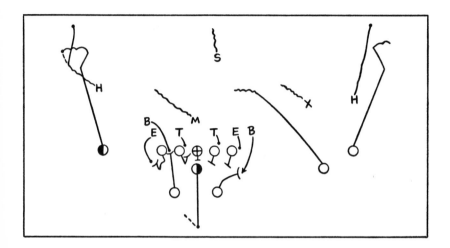

Diagram 9-1

In diagram 9-2 the quarterback has called Right-55 circle. His key on the safety alerts him to work to the formation side. As he drops back into the pocket, his read on the "X" man indicates man coverage, so he sets up and drills the ball to his circling split end inside of the linebacker.

Diagram 9-3 illustrates Right-55 post. Again, the quarterback's key dictates he must work toward formation. As he reads the "X" man on his way back to set up, he is aware of some type of zone coverage. His response is to stay with the wingback circling to the inside. The quarterback may have to hold the ball a moment longer to allow the wingback to work to an open spot between the linebackers. The "X" man may cover the deep one-third, the short outside one-fourth, or back straight up in a four-across zone. The only read on the "X" man that will prevent the quarterback from throwing to the wingback is the man-for-man coverage as shown in diagram 9-2. It is then a matter of common sense to pass to the split end because he definitely will have only single coverage.

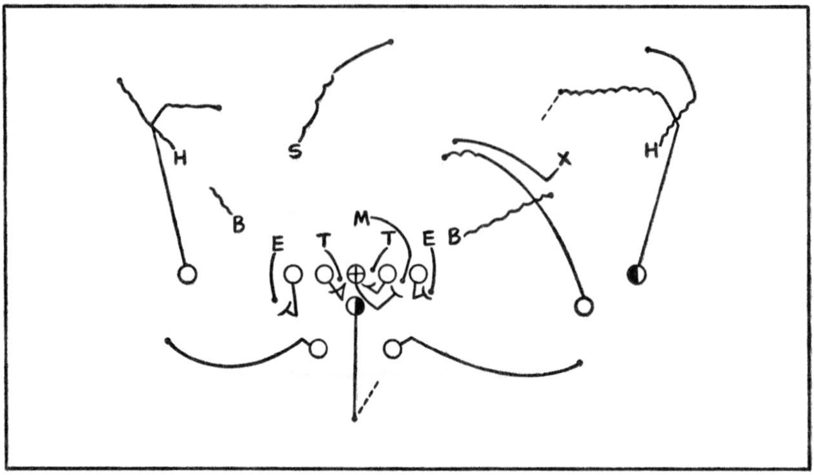

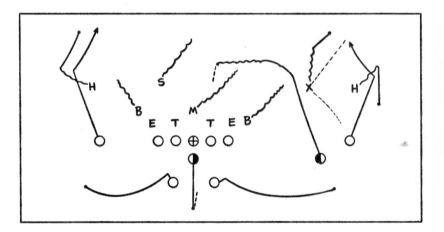

Diagram 9-2

Diagram 9-3

In diagram 9-4, the quarterback's key indicates he will be passing to his tight end on the called Right-55 circle. However, the outside linebacker drops back to shut out the circle throwing lane. The quarterback reacts to this by passing to his flaring tailback. The tailback is released when his assignment does not rush.

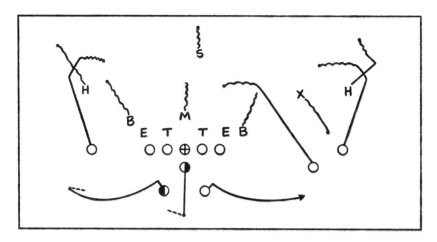

Diagram 9-4

READING THREE ON TWO

There are several ways three defenders might attempt to play the two wide receivers on the formation side, but the end result is always in favor of the offense by reading man or zone coverage. The tip-off is the linebacker or whomever the defense aligns over the wingback. In diagrams 9-5 and 9-6, the key directs the quarterback to the formation side. When three defenders appear on that side, the quarterback reads the defender playing on the wingback. The wingback must take an inside release even if the defender is aligned to the wingback's inside. The wingback in that case takes an inside flat release across the face of the defender before breaking upfield for his circle route. In diagram 9-5, the defender sticks on the wingback which indicates man coverage and allows the quarterback to pass to either his split end or his fullback flaring to that side.

In diagram 9-6, the defender playing over the wingback drops into zone coverage, freeing the wingback to receive the circle pass.

Other pass combinations or individual routes will be discussed later in this chapter to illustrate combatting the three coverage on the formation side. However, when three defenders are required against the passing game on the formation side, the defense becomes vulnerable to the Triple Option.

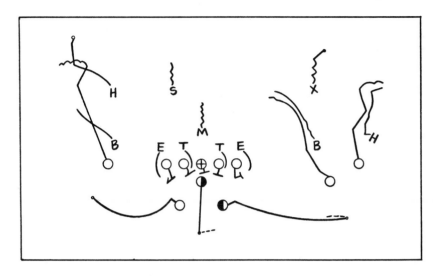

Diagram 9-5

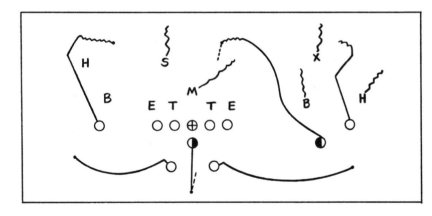

Diagram 9-6

THE EIGHT-MAN FRONT

On rare occasions, an opponent will defend with an eight-man front. This is suicide for the defense, but, nevertheless, the offense must be prepared always against the unusual to be able to take advantage of whatever weakness is available.

The eight-man front alignment allows only three secondary men to cover the wide scope of the Cincinnati formation. They become vulnerable in many areas, but most glaringly on the quick side. The wide spread of the wingback and split end forces the safety to move to the formation side, leaving open the deep middle. This puts a tremendous burden on the defensive halfback covering the tight end. The defensive halfback cannot cover a receiver from the flag to the goalpost consistently. Sooner or later he will get burned. (See diagram 9-7.)

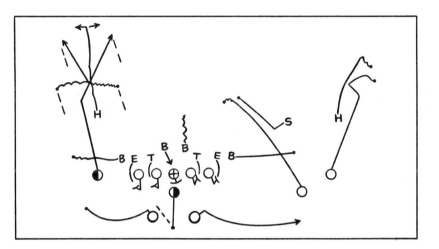

Diagram 9-7

The eight-man front forces the defense to play man-for-man coverage which is like skating on thin ice. The only way for the eight-man front to succeed is to rush all eight men with hopes of putting the quarterback on the ground. Therefore, to counterattack this maneuver the offense must have a "hot" receiver. The quick side has four blockers, so it can stop the four rushers on that side. However, on the strong side, the fullback is assigned to both the linebacker and the outside rusher. Should both of them rush, the outside rusher will be free. The quarterback then becomes responsible for the unblocked rusher. The wingback, aware of this situation, will shorten his path on the inside release circle route to a flatter course, yelling "hot-hot-hot" as he sprints to the inside. The quarterback can stop at a shorter distance in his retreat and drop the wingback the ball for a successful play. (See diagram 9-8.)

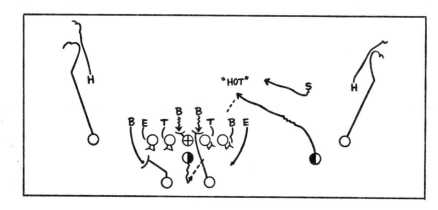

Diagram 9-8

Should the opponent continue to rush eight and cover with only three, the offense should go into "Stay" protection on the strong side and throw individual routes to the tight end until the cows come home. (See diagram 9-9.)

THE COMBINATIONS

Once the basic plan (55) is established, other passing combinations can be utilized. The basic plan enables the coach in the press box to pick out exactly how the defense is covering. This makes it a simple job to fit the combination to the situation.

QUICKSIDE COMBINATIONS

When the safety aligns in spot no. 3, this allows the passing game to be directed to the tight-end side. The combination involves the tight end and the tailback. By utilizing the tailback, the offense has inserted flare control.

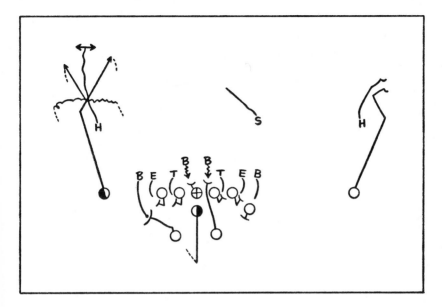

Diagram 9-9

PASS 59

Pass 59 illustrates the tight end and tailback working together. When an inside route is called (post or circle), the tailback sprints to the flat, gaining a depth of no more than five yards. His path pulls the linebacker outside for the quarterback to have a clear passing lane. (See diagram 9-10.)

In diagram 9-11, the tight end runs the outside cuts while the tailback turns up inside, holding the linebacker there.

The path of the tailback controls the linebacker. Should the linebacker blitz, the quarterback must dump the ball to the tailback. The tailback must see the linebacker coming on his first few steps and be ready to receive the pass from the quarterback. (See diagram 9-12.)

By working with only the few basic cuts, you can install any number of combinations without complications. Pass 59 post, circle, or bend can be called. This indicates the tight end should run the called route with the tailback providing the clearing action.

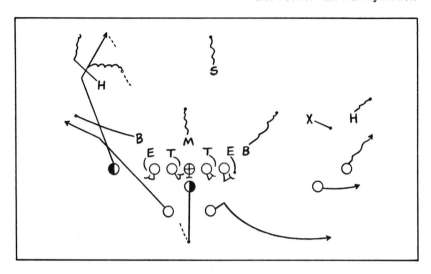

Diagram 9-10

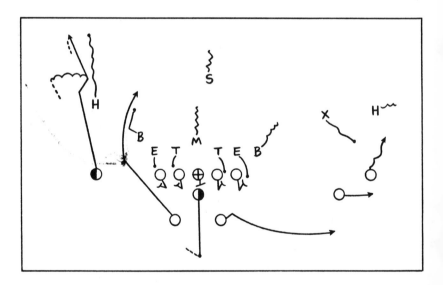

Diagram 9-11

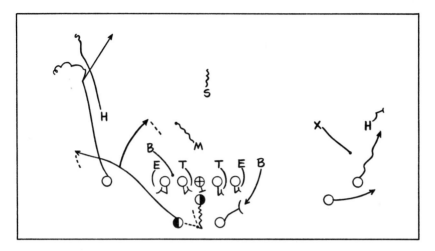

Diagram 9-12

PASS 58

When the coach wants the tight end and tailback combination without concern about the linebacker blitzing, he calls pass 58. Pass 58 adds to the protection to insure the opportunity for the quarterback to set up without concern about blitzing linebackers. The fullback takes the tailback's block of pass 55 and the wingback closes in for "stay" protection on the strong side. (See diagram 9-13.)

The same basic cuts (post, circle, bend) are called for pass 58 with the added protection measures. When 58 circle is called and the defensive halfback turns his feet to the inside to cover the tight end, another route must be added—called 58 take-off. (See diagram 9-14.) This pass alerts the tailback to read the feet of the defensive halfback. If the defender's feet turn inside to cover the tight end, the tailback breaks down the sideline looking for the long arch. The quarterback also reads the feet of the defender. If the feet turn inside, the quarterback is ready to heave the long bomb. Should the defender's feet stay outside, the quarterback goes to the tight end for the circle route between the linebackers.

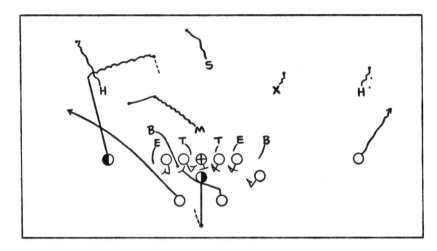

Diagram 9-13

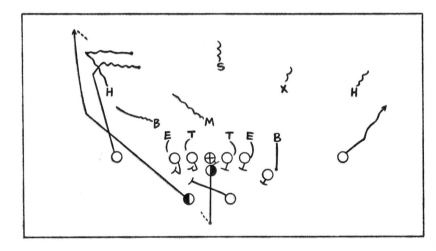

Diagram 9-14

PASS 57

There will come a time when one will still want to throw to the tight-end side regardless of the coverage. This can be accomplished by calling pass 57. Pass 57 adds a three-out pattern to the quick side providing the quickside linebacker does not blitz. (See diagram 9-15.) The fullback flares to the quick side while the tailback takes his pass 55 assignment. Should the linebacker blitz, the tailback must block him. (See diagram 9-16.)

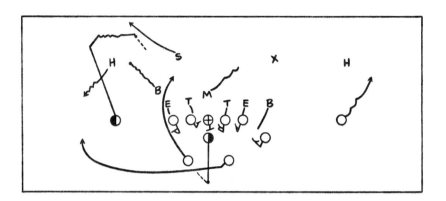

Diagram 9-15

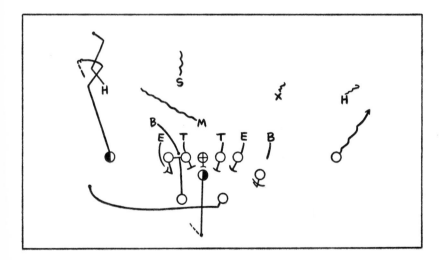

Diagram 9-16

The same basic passes (post, circle, bend) can be used for pass 57. "Stay" protection is needed for security on the strong side.

Pass 57 circle is very effective versus the 6-5 goal-line defense. The five linebackers are assigned man-for-man coverage. The linebacker on the fullback has a most difficult assignment. (See diagram 9-17.)

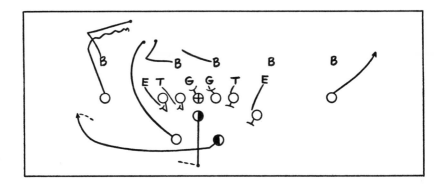

Diagram 9-17

PASS 56

Pass 56 completes the pocket quickside passes. It is the same as pass 59 except the tailback flares to the outside for the pass called to the tight end. Should the linebacker blitz, the quarterback must dump the ball to the tailback. (See diagram 9-18.)

STRONGSIDE COMBINATIONS

The strongside pocket passes are numbered 51, 52, 53, and 54.

PASS 51

Pass 51 is designed to throw to the split end with the wingback running clearing action similar to the tailback's for the tight end (pass 59). When an outside route is called (bend, flag, etc.), the wingback runs a tight circle. (See diagram 9-19.) The fullback runs

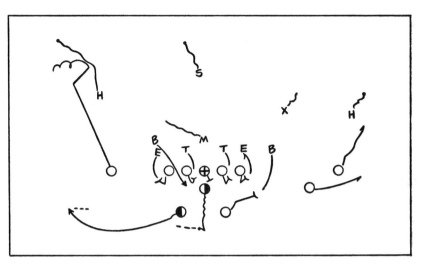

Diagram 9-18

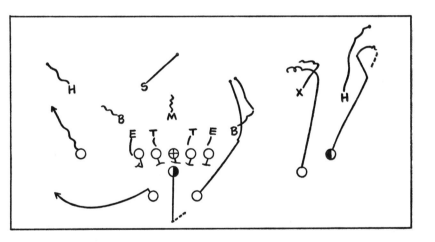

Diagram 9-19

a gut route inside. This is a flare control on the linebacker. Should the linebacker blitz, the quarterback must dump the ball to the fullback.

When the split end runs the inside cuts, the wingback, because of his alignment close to the split end, must sprint downfield four steps before breaking into the flat. (See diagram 9-20.)

When the safety lines up in position number one, it allows the quarterback to work individual routes to the split end by calling pass 51 and to the wingback by calling pass 52.

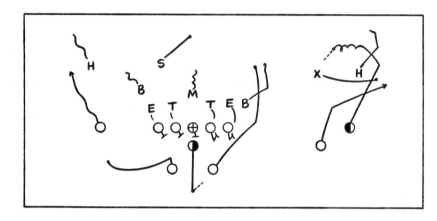

Diagram 9-20

PASS 52

Two individual routes were especially effective for the wingback at Cincinnati: the bend and flag cuts. When pass 52 bend was called, it was necessary for the split end to run a post route to clear out the defensive halfback. The fullback continued to run the gut pattern for flare control on the linebacker. The wingback ran the bend route exactly as a wide receiver. (See diagram 9-21.)

When pass 52 flag was called, the split end ran a quick-out or loafed off the line to pull the defensive halfback upfield. (See diagram 9-22.)

PASS 53

Pass 53 can be utilized against any type coverage. This pass involves the split end and the fullback working together as a

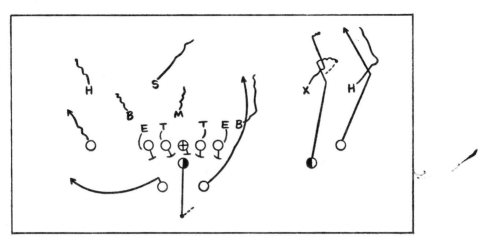

Diagram 9-21

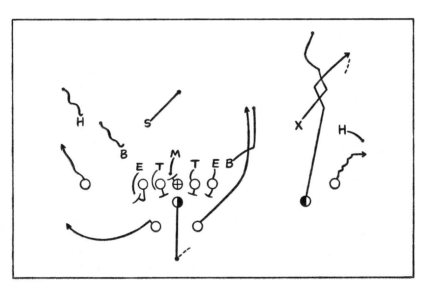

Diagram 9-22

combination. When the split end runs an inside route, the fullback runs the clearing action to the outside. (See diagram 9-23.)

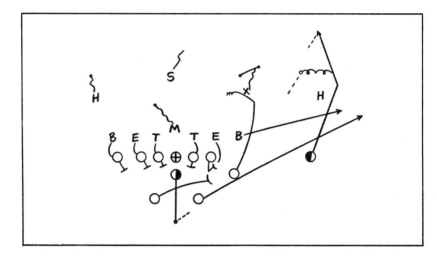

Diagram 9-23

It is necessary in pass 53 for the tight end to close tight for "stay" protection on the quick side. "Stay" protection allows the tailback to pick up the fullback's blocking assignment. The wingback should close tight and run a circle pattern to the inside to hold the inside linebackers.

PASS 54

Pass 54 is a method used to get four receivers out to one side. The split end and wingback work together as in pass 51. The fullback takes his 55 assignment. Should the linebacker not blitz, the fullback is free to run a gut route to hold the linebackers inside. The tailback flares to the strong side to force short outside coverage or be completely open. The tight end must close in for "stay" protection on the quick side. (See diagram 9-24.)

55-UNDER

A special pass that was added to the Cincinnati passing game to combat the two-deep coverages was the "under" pattern—a type of pick.

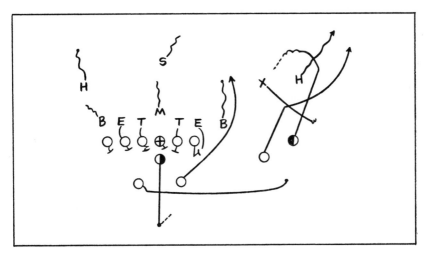

Diagram 9-24

On two-deep coverages, each safety covers one-half of the deep zone. Five other defenders must then cover the five potential receivers short.

In diagram 9-25, the linebackers and halfbacks are covering man-for-man. The call is Right-55 under. The split end loafs off

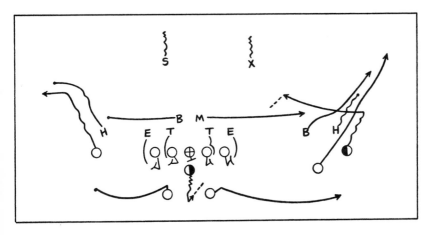

Diagram 9-25

the line as the wingback clears between split end and defender. As the clearing action takes place, the split end breaks underneath to the inside. The fullback checks the linebacker for a blitz, then sprints toward the sideline pulling the linebacker out of the middle. The tailback pulls his linebacker out to the quick side, leaving the big hole in the middle. After conquering the sprint back, the quarterback learns to back-pedal for his setting-up in order to throw to his left better on certain occasions. The back-pedal technique is best for this particular pass because he can stop quickly when the split end slips into the open and fire the ball to him at that moment.

The large opening in the middle should also be used to advantage by the wingback in running an inside route with an outside stick. (See diagram 9-26.)

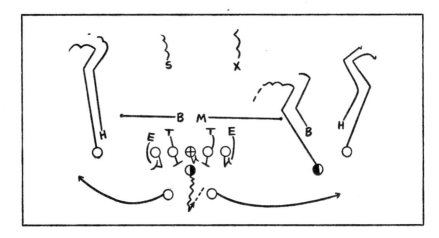

Diagram 9-26

When the five underneath defenders play zone, the wingback comes open as a regular 55 or one of the wide receivers does in a bend route or one of the backs flaring. (See diagram 9-27.)

However, again I must point out this defensive arrangement restricts the defense versus the Triple Option by becoming vulnerable to the handoff and presenting a soft corner for the pitch or keep.

There are many combinations and situations in the passing game and with just a few basic patterns, the offense can spend its valuable time on technique and exploit the many ways to get the ball to the receiver.

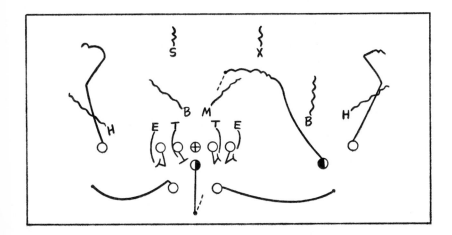

Diagram 9-27

Although the "plan" offers much flexibility in the passing game, it is never complete without draws and screens to control the rush in certain areas.

THE DRAWS

The draw can be an effective call versus the hard inside rush. Normally, the draw is called on first or second down. However, it can also be effective at times on third and long. I shall never forget our (Oklahoma) game with Nebraska in 1966 on national television. We were behind 9-7 with only one minute remaining. We had the ball on Nebraska's thirty-five, third down and eight. An incomplete pass meant we would have to go for a field goal (52 yards). We called a draw. The fullback broke into the clear down to Nebraska's 10-yard line. We moved the ball closer to use up a little more time and then kicked an easy field goal to win the big game 10-9.

At Cincinnati we put our draw into the 57-54 blocking scheme and could draw to either the fullback or the tailback. The only difference in the blocking scheme was the technique for the center and guards.

In diagram 9-28, right 57 fullback is called. This indicates a draw play to the fullback with 57 protection. It also alerts the center and quick guard of their technique responsibilities. Versus an even defense, the fullback draw will be directed over the quick guard as in diagram 9-28. Against an odd defense, it will be over center (diagram 9-29). When over the quick guard (versus the even defense), he must drop back two steps with his shoulders square to the line of scrimmage. This is different from his pass protection technique of dropping back to the inside. For the draw, the quick guard wants the rusher to declare his rush, to either side. Then the quick guard must block him in that direction. The quarterback drops back into the pocket handing the ball to the fullback as he passes him. The fullback sets, facing his blocking assignment with his inside elbow high for the handoff. As the ball is handed to the fullback, he must read the quick guard's block and break through the side opposite.

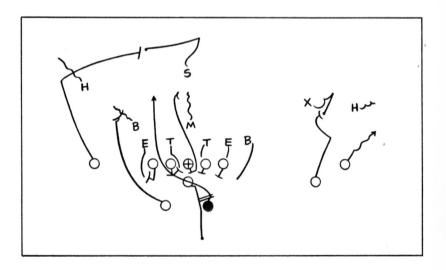

Diagram 9-28

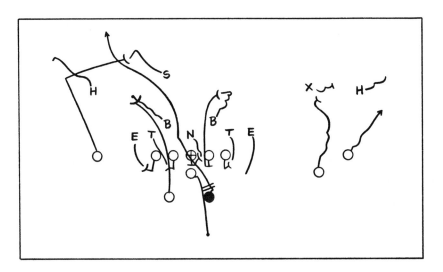

Diagram 9-29

The tailback is assigned to the quickside linebacker. He first checks for a blitz. If it does not occur, he allows the linebacker to drop off the line before he attacks. Just prior to the quarterback going passed the tailback on his retreat into the pocket, the tailback sprints toward the quick linebacker, taking the easiest and most convenient path to block him downfield.

The strong guard and tackle block no. 1 and no. 2, respectively, as they do in "stay" protection. When the strong guard has a linebacker to block, he first checks the blitz. If it does not occur, he allows the linebacker to drop off the line considerably before attacking. The same is true for the center versus a middle linebacker.

Fifty-four tailback draw is just the opposite from 57 fullback. The quick side blocks "stay" protection with the strong guard and center using the square-shoulder technique for the tailback to break off the block.

THE POCKET SCREENS

The screens used at Cincinnati were also simple, but with variety and flexibility. They were used to control or slow down the outside rushes and were normally called on second or third down.

As on the draws, the pass number called correlates with the protection. The first screen is 57 screen-left tailback. This means the ball will be faked to the fullback to simulate the draw. After faking, the quarterback continues back into the pocket, looks downfield, then turns to the quick side to pick out his tailback.

The blocking scheme is simple. Everyone blocks the 57 rule. The tackles are instructed to stay with their blocks. The guards and center stay with their blocks for three counts (one thousand one, one thousand two, one thousand three), then release to the quick side. The quick guard blocks the first man coming up from the outside such as the defensive halfback. If the defensive halfback fails to show, the quick guard turns upfield and blocks the first defender he approaches. The center sprints laterally to the quick side, and peels back to the inside to block the first pursuer from the inside. The strong guard's first responsibility is picking up any defender who is a threat to the tailback before he can start downfield. If this does not occur, the strong guard should turn downfield and lead the tailback, blocking the first different-colored jersey that approaches. (See diagram 9-30.)

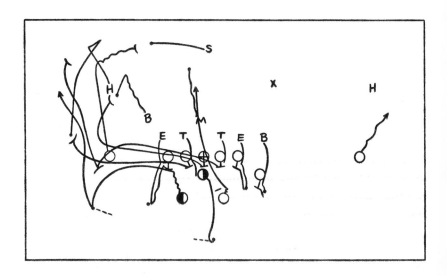

Diagram 9-30

Fifty-three screen-left tight end can be called for a screen to the tight end to slow down a strong outside rush when the tight end is utilized for "stay" protection.

In diagram 9-31, 51 screen-right fullback is called. This call results in a fake draw to the tailback and a screen to the right for the guards and center. The strong guard now picks up the widest threat with the quick guard leading the way for the fullback.

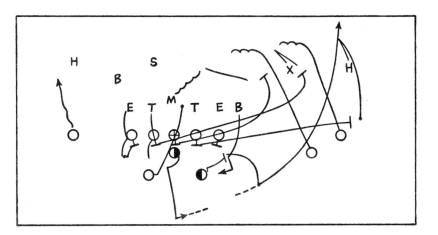

Diagram 9-31

The Cincinnati passing game was simple to execute, but had much variety and flexibility. However, it must be thoroughly understood that the plan (55) should be established before additional wrinkles are added. Once the plan goes into effect, it is a simple matter to pick out the defensive tendencies. Once the coach nails down the defense's intention as to coverage, he can pick a combination to work against it. Should the coverage change, he can call the combination that best fits the new one. Should there be any doubt, it is a simple matter to go back to the plan and start again. I am sure the reader gets the message that it is important to have a plan upon which to rely.

The opportunity to work with an excellent passing game is one of the biggest thrills I have experienced in my coaching career. The ball in the air is a great equalizer and makes the game fun to coach.

Ten

CHECK-WITH-ME
SYSTEM AND STRATEGY

The tactical department is the most interesting area of the football program. After everything is put together, the question of great importance is when and where does it apply. The Triple Option and pocket pass combination affords the biggest opportunity for an offense to succeed.

Elimination of individual mistakes is the surest way to keep a drive moving. One mistake will break a drive and often result in poor field position. It is almost impossible to win the tough game without maintaining adequate field position.

We stop ourselves in various ways—wrong play called against a strong segment of the defense, a missed assignment, missed block, fumble, penalty or interception.

Many coaches spend hour upon hour training their quarterbacks to select intelligently the best play for a particular situation. He is taught to recognize defensive tendencies, along with an understanding of the intricacies of offensive standards, and then to attack one segment or one man in the defense.

The quarterback will have many training aids available: the down and distance charts, the vertical and horizontal zones, press box advice, and other situation tendencies. Even if he has made the best selection possible, when he arrives at the line of scrimmage, the defense may not be what he expected.

To offset this negative factor, we believed at Cincinnati in setting up the "Check-with-Me" system. This system and overall strategy must go hand-in-hand. This is my reason for putting the two topics together in this chapter.

CHECK-WITH-ME

The "Check-with-Me" is a method used to call the play on the line of scrimmage. It can be introduced by two methods. First, the quarterback in the huddle can call the formation and "Check-with-Me," then break the huddle. This indicates the play will be called on the line of scrimmage. Second, the quarterback can call a formation ("Right-Right-Right") for his team to line up in without a huddle. Anytime the quarterback uses this method, it is understood the team will line up immediately in the formation called without a huddle. Furthermore, it is understood the play will be called on the line of scrimmage. Whichever method is used, the ball will be snapped on the third sound.

The basic "Check-with-Me" system involves the Triple Option (71-79) and play-action passes 22 and 28. Along with (pass) 55 (post, circle, bend), this gives the coach a built-in game plan each week.

These line-of-scrimmage calls are very practical for exploiting the weakest segment of the defense.

On the line, the quarterback puts the team down with the quick sound and starts the numbers. The numbers are now live. The number called will be the play. For example, "Hike (quick sound), seventy-one, seventy-one, Hike-Hike-Hike." The 71 is repeated to be sure each side of the line heard the play.

THE DIRECTION

On the line, the quarterback must first decide upon direction, then make the decision to run or pass. This is handled very simply. The direction (to formation or away) is determined by the alignment of the safety. This is the same key used by the quarterback to pick out his receiver in the 55 pass plan.

The Cincinnati formation helps the quarterback pick out his key. The three spots in which the safety may line up were explained in chapter two. If the safety is aligned in spot number one, the play must be directed toward formation. When the safety is lined up in spot number-three, the play must be directed away from formation. When he is in spot number two, it depends upon the location of the football. Should the ball be on the hash mark, the safety should be considered in spot number one. When it is between hash marks, he should be considered in spot number three.

DECISION—RUN OR PASS

With the safety in spot number one, (play toward formation), whether to run Triple 71 or play-action pass 22 is determined by counting the number of defenders covering the two wide receivers. By imagining a line between our strong tackle and the wingback, the quarterback can easily identify the coverage.

If three defenders are aligned in the area with our two wide receivers, the quarterback will call 71. (See diagram 10-1.) When only two defenders line up in the outside area, the quarterback is instructed to call play-action pass 22. (See diagram 10-2.)

In diagram 10-1, the defense is vulnerable to the Triple because it has left the defensive end to stop the handoff and softened the corner for the pitch or keep because of the displacement of the outside linebacker.

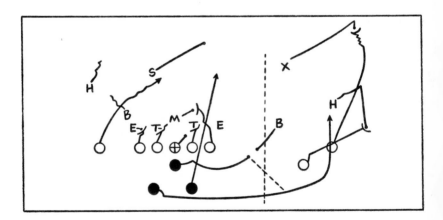

Diagram 10-1

In diagram 10-2, the defense has tightened up to stop the Triple, thus becoming vulnerable to pass 22.

As previously mentioned, when the safety moves to the middle or favors the formation in spot number three, the play direction must be away from formation. Again we go to the counting method to determine run or pass. If the tight end has single coverage, the quarterback will call pass 28. (See diagram 10-3.) When two defenders cover him, Triple 79 must be called. (See diagram 10-4.)

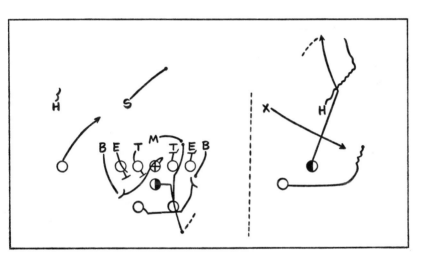

Diagram 10-2

In diagram 10-3, the defense is vulnerable to the pass because of single coverage on our tight end. Refer back to chapter six (Triple Play-Action Passes) for the execution of passes 22 and 28.

In diagram 10-4, the defense has placed two defenders outside to cover our tight end; therefore, it has softened the Triple area for the handoff, keep, or pitch.

UNORTHODOX DEFENSES

Occasionally the defense will align in an unusual arrangement such as in diagrams 10-5 and 10-6. Whenever our quarterback

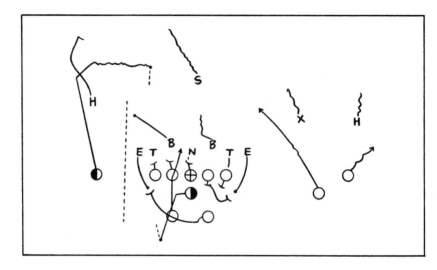

Diagram 10-3

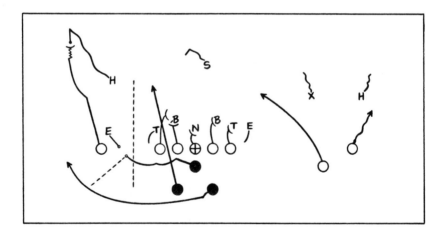

Diagram 10-4

came upon a situation he could not recognize, he was instructed to call for the quarterback sneak with wedge blocking (15-15). This kept him out of trouble until he could get help from the press box.

In diagram 10-5, the situation should be handled with run 79. Although the key indicates direction should be toward formation, the defense has three men playing the pass and three more on the line to formation side. But it has sacrificed the quick side, with only two linemen to defend versus the run.

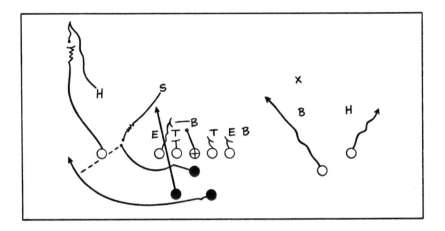

Diagram 10-5

In diagram 10-6, the key indicates direction away from formation. However, the defense has double coverage on the quick side along with three defenders on the line to stop the Triple. Therefore, the quarterback would call 71 toward the formation because only two defenders are on the line to stop the Triple.

The "Check-with-Me" is an excellent system. Along with 55 it is your game plan each week and a superior method in training the quarterback in recognizing defenses and their vulnerable areas. See diagram 10-7 for all the possible results from a simple key. This system enables the quarterback to select the best play after recognition.

The "Check-with-Me" system is simple and foolproof. I was never completely satisfied with the type of automatic system of calling one play in the huddle then changing at the line. I believe this interferes with concentration and curtails a player's aggressiveness. When the player does not have a play until he gets to the line of scrimmage, he will concentrate more on the defensive tendencies. This keeps him alert and ready, and does not diminish his natural aggressiveness.

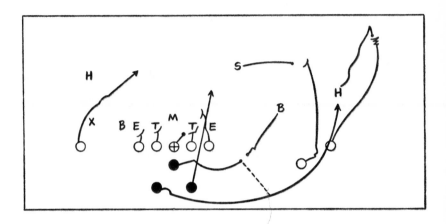

Diagram 10-6

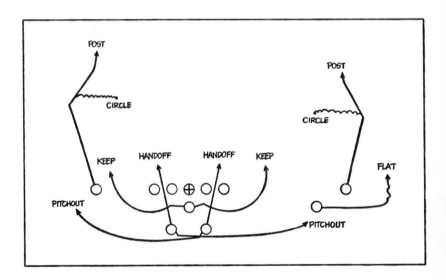

Diagram 10-7

Any series of plays can be worked into the "Check-with-Me." As long as the quarterback has a simple key to work with, he can master the system in a relatively short time. This system helps the quarterback understand defensive tendencies better than any other aid.

THE STRATEGY

Strategy is first organized into four basic zones: the backed-up zone, the minus zone, the plus zone, and the going-in zone.

The backed-up zone is when the offense has the ball inside its own five-yard line. The minus zone is from the five to the 50-yard line. The plus zone is from the 50 to the opponent's ten. The going-in zone is inside the ten.

Strategy must also be grouped into degrees of actions. This means a good many elements affect the decisions that must be made. Score, time remaining, down and distance to go, and weather conditions are main considerations. Therefore, in discussing each zone, the various elements must be taken into consideration.

THE BACKED-UP ZONE

The backed-up zone is the most dangerous. Giving up the football in this zone is committing hari-kari. When your offense takes over in this zone, it must have one thought—move the ball out to the five-yard line. If this mission is accomplished, the offense will be able to line up in spread punt formation on the punting down. This is very important. In spread punt, the punter aligns at least 14 yards from the center. The ball needs to be on the five-yard line in order not to push the punter too close to the end line.

Should the offense not be able to move the ball out to the five-yard line, this means a tight punt situation in which the punter can only retreat nine to 10 yards from the center. The spread punt will give the offense the best coverage and cut down the return yardage because the members of the nine-man front block through their assignments releasing immediately for coverage.

When it is necessary to utilize tight punt formation, the linemen must block until the ball is punted before releasing, thus allowing the safety man an opportunity for a longer return.

Giving up yardage on the minus side of the 50-yard line because of the difference of punting formations is the significant factor involved in understanding why it is important to move the ball out to or beyond the five-yard line.

GIVING UP A SAFETY

There is such a difference that when the offense must line up in tight punt, it should consider giving up a safety and punt or placekick from the 20-yard line. This can be justified only when two points do not matter. By predicting the results of each punt formation and comparing them, the value of this suggestion can be shown. From the five-yard line the spread punt will be approximately 40 yards. This means the safety will receive the punt on our 45-yard line. The coverage should be good enough to hold him to no more than a five-yard return. This places the ball on the 40-yard line. Now let's examine the tight punt kicked to our 45-yard line. The coverage will arrive at least 1.5 seconds later, allowing the safety a return of approximately 15 yards, putting the ball on the 30-yard line. A difference of 10 yards in this zone is a distinct difference.

Giving up a safety is easy. From tight punt, the snap goes to the punter, who then runs beyond the end line. Free punting or placekicking from the 20-yard line enables the offense to get the ball across the 50-yard line. Two points sometimes is a small price to pay to help stop opponents from scoring as many as eight.

Giving up a safety can be used in other situations as well. A strong wind in the punter's face or a slippery ball due to wet weather can be reasons for the intentional safety. It can be used late in the game when you are behind to gain better field position or when you are ahead and two points matters less than using up the clock. In the latter case, the punter should take the long snap and run back and forth in the end zone and step out just before he is touched by the chasers. It might be wise to substitute the quarterback in this situation.

THE MINUS ZONE

The minus zone (our 5 to midfield) we considered a three-down zone. This meant we would punt on fourth down.

Our objective in the minus zone was to cross the 50-yard line. This can be accomplished by running, passing, or punting. It is very important to never give up the ball on your side of the 50-yard line.

Over the years, records have been kept on this vital point. The records are proof that the team which gives up the ball on its side of the 50 more than its opponents will lose. Although this is a percentage observation, it will invariably hold up over a season.

Each team will have the football from 12 to 15 drives per game in today's football. This figure became more flexible when the rules-makers of intercollegiate football injected the new rule of stopping the clock when a first down is made until the chains have been moved. This prolongs the game, giving each team an opportunity to have possession more times. Assuming each team will have 15 opportunities to start a drive, the positions from which each shall begin its drives often determine the ball game. For example, Team A has 15 opportunities, five of which start on the opponent's side of the 50. Team B also has 15, but only two begin on the opponent's half. Based on the theory of where the drive begins, Team A should be the winner, and over a season this will prove true more often than not.

The kicking game plus the elimination of offensive mistakes plays an important role in gaining the best field position. Therefore, in the minus zone the objective is to move the ball across the 50-yard line either by running, passing, or kicking—DO NOT GIVE UP THE BALL ON YOUR SIDE OF THE 50-YARD LINE.

THE PLUS ZONE

Once possession is gained inside the plus zone, the objective is to score. Should the offense not be able to score, the objective is to give the opponents possession in poor field position. If the offense can cross midfield and keep its opponents backed up, eventually the field-position theory will pay dividends.

The game should be called the same in the plus zone as in the minus zone. The situations for the first three downs are the same. The difference comes on fourth down. In the minus zone, the offense punts to get the ball across the 50-yard line; in the plus zone, to back the opponents against their goal line. Therefore, fourth down in the plus zone is considered a bonus down. Three decisions are available at this point. Go for the first down, attempt a field goal, or punt the ball inside the 10-yard line. The yard line will usually determine if a field goal attempt is practical. The ability of the field goal kicker is the deciding factor. The kicker may be effective from the 30-yard line. This means anytime the ball crosses the 30-yard line and a fourth down comes up, the field goal can be called. If the ball is outside the 30-yard line, it is wise to punt. Going for a first down must depend upon the yards to go and the need for a first down at that particular time. The score, time remaining, and weather will determine this call. Should the offense decide to go for a first down, it must consider the yards to go in determining the type of play called. If the situation is fourth and three or more yards, it would be wise to select a 55 pass, screen, or draw. If the situation is two yards or less, the offense should call upon its best running play.

The field goal can be a tremendous weapon. Three points on the scoreboard are better than zero. Jimmy O'Brien at Cincinnati was effective inside the 25-yard line. With the goal posts located on the end line for intercollegiate football and the holder seven yards behind his center, this requires a kick of 42 yards. Occasionally, Jimmy was allowed to attempt longer yardage and was successful on two 47-yard attempts.

The formation for the field goal requires the team to hold its blocks until the ball is place-kicked. After the ball is kicked the signal is given by the holder to "cover-cover-cover." This is to remind the team that the field goal like a punt can be returned.

Inside the plus zone but outside field-goal range, whether to punt depends also upon the ability of the punter. Some punters can "sky" the ball and still drop it inside the 10-yard line, allowing the team to sprint downfield and stop the roll within a few yards of the goal line. The ends and up-backs are given the responsibility of face guarding the goal line while the guards and center must stop in front of the safety to make sure he is not receiving the punt. The tackles sprint to the ball.

If field-goal range is from the 20-yard line or closer it would be unwise to punt from just outside the 20-yard line. Should the ball roll into the end zone for a touchback and be brought out to the 20-yard line, it would mean a punt of only a few yards. Should this be the case, it would be wise to go for the first down. The punt out of bounds inside the 10-yard line is another consideration, but it is difficult for a punter to be effective in both the "sky" and the "flag" punting technique. It is best to take only one method and perfect it.

THE GOING-IN ZONE

Once the ball moves inside the opponent's 10-yard line, the offense is located in the going-in zone. The zone is definitely considered a four-down one. With the ball on the 10-yard line, the offense must average two and one-half yards a play to score. The reason I make a point of this is the third down and five yards to go situation. If the offense will not panic by attempting to get all five yards on third down, it will have a better opportunity to score on fourth down. A play that will gain 2½ yards or slightly more will keep the consistency rate working and allow the offense to come up with a fourth and two and a half yards or less instead of a fourth and five-yard situation.

When the fourth down situation arrives, the decision must be made whether to go for the touchdown or the field goal. If there are two yards or less to go for the touchdown, I recommend going for it. With more than two yards and when three points will tie or take the lead in the game, I suggest the field-goal attempt. If three points will not tie or take the lead, I suggest going for the touchdown. If it fails, the opponents have the ball backed up inside their 10-yard line. A good defense and a good punt return will project the offense back again knocking on the opponents' door.

The fourth down situation in the going-in zone when the offense goes for the touchdown is perhaps the most tense moment in the football game. This is where Bud Wilkinson's favorite expression, "football is a game of inches," becomes a statement with real meaning. The touchdown has such a strong psychological effect, it is unbelievable the confidence the scoring team can generate. On the other hand, if the defense holds, the psychology is reversed.

Jerry Claiborne, a superb coach, is a master in teaching goal-line defense. Jerry has perhaps the best record of all coaches in stopping the opponent inside the 10-yard line. Coach Claiborne did a great selling job with his teams—convincing them they could always stop the opponent inside the 10-yard line. This is also the approach the offensive coach must take in working with his squad. The offense must always believe it can score anytime it reaches the going-in zone.

THE EXTRA POINT

After the touchdown comes the most important play in football—the extra point. Should the situation dictate going for two points, we would select the best play from our going-in attack or fake the placekick and run or pass for the two pointer. In many instances we would ask the official to move the ball to the left hashmark to take advantage of a certain defense. If the one point is needed, the placekicking formation is called the same as for the field goal. The one exception, of course, is that it is not necessary to cover this attempt. However, it is important to have an outlet in case of a bad snap. If our holder mishandled the ball or received a bad snap from the center and was unable to set the ball on the kicking tee for the placekicker, he yelled "fire-fire-fire" (Coach Paul Bryant's terminology). He picked the ball up and sprinted either to the left or right side, whichever was more convenient, and ran or passed to the open receiver.

In strategy planning, the coach must prepare for the complete game. Therefore, other factors must be considered: the two-minute offense, stopping-the-clock, running-out-the-clock, and scouting your own offense.

THE TWO-MINUTE OFFENSE

The two-minute offense can be used with two minutes remaining in the first half, or two minutes remaining to play in the game.

In the first half when you are ahead, run out the clock. When you are behind one or two touchdowns with the ball behind your own 35-yard line—run out the clock. This will avoid the possibility of going into the locker room three touchdowns behind. When you are behind one or more touchdowns and have the ball beyond your own 35-yard line, go into the two-minute offense.

The two-minute offense is a hurry-up one, always used when you are behind with less than two minutes to play in the game regardless where the ball is situated.

When the signal comes from the bench to the quarterback to go into the two-minute attack, he immediately orders the team to line up in a formation without a huddle. The quarterback always calls the formation toward the widest side of the field. For example, the ball is placed close to the left hashmark. The quarterback must respond by calling "right-right-right." This will align the team in right formation. The quarterback will call the play on the line of scrimmage. He quickly puts the team down on the quick sound, calls the play once, repeats the call, then starts the cadence for the third sound.

STOP-THE-CLOCK

Rather than take a chance of time running out, the quarter-back calls for "Big Ben—Big Ben—Big Ben." This is a procedure that will handle the situation when no more time-outs are available. The team quickly lines up in a football position. The ball is snapped on the quick sound. The wide receiver on the shorter side runs a hitch. The quarterback throws the ball over the receiver's head and out of bounds to stop the clock. This uses up a down but may save the game.

The two-minute attack is a dramatic maneuver that can pull game after game out of the fire. Hypothetical situations must be practiced time and time again so the team will be prepared when they are faced with the crisis.

RUN-OUT-THE-CLOCK

The one situation with which every coach likes to be faced is running out the clock with less than two minutes to play in the game. This is a happy moment, but the situation must be practiced thoroughly to keep it happy.

It is important to run plays that will "eat up" the clock. The plays must be the safest available and the ball carrier must be instructed not to go out of bounds and stop the clock. With two minutes remaining and providing the defense does not call time-out to stop the clock, the offense should use up approximately 35 seconds on each of the first three downs. This can be accomplished because the team is allowed 25 seconds after the official marks the ball ready for play before the ball must be snapped. Assuming the offense uses up 20 seconds before the snap, runs a wide play to take up time, gets up slow off the ball to delay the official giving the ready-to-play signal, the team can easily use up the 35 seconds. If this is accomplished during the first three downs, the offense can remain in the huddle on fourth down and allow the clock to run out.

One method we used at Cincinnati was very effective. The quarterback called "clock-clock-clock." This brought the team to the line of scrimmage in a tight formation. As the team was positioning on the line of scrimmage, the quarterback kept check on the official's signal for ready-to-play. Once the signal was given, the quarterback began a countdown out loud so his teammates could hear, "25-24-23-22," and so on down to 5. When he reached the number 5 he called "Hike"; the ball was snapped and the quarterback sneak executed. The official had to be right because he was being checked by the quarterback on his countdown. Also, the defense often became impatient and charged offside to stop the clock but gave us a five-yard gain without loss of a down.

SCOUTING OFFENSE

To complete strategy planning, the offense should be scouted each game by someone other than a staff member. At Cincinnati, I had a former football coach scout us as he would an opponent. He turned over to us each week the scouting report. This was very similar to the report our opponents would have compiled. If the coach will give his opponent credit for being prepared, he will realize he must not let any single item on the checklist of things to be covered daily slip by. Complete preparation for the upcoming game will be the deciding factor in victory over defeat.

Index